Williamsburg at War

Virginia's Colonial Capital in the Revolutionary War

Michael Cecere

HERITAGE BOOKS
2023

HERITAGE BOOKS

AN IMPRINT OF HERITAGE BOOKS, INC.

Books, CDs, and more—Worldwide

For our listing of thousands of titles see our website
at
www.HeritageBooks.com

Published 2023 by
HERITAGE BOOKS, INC.
Publishing Division
5810 Ruatan Street
Berwyn Heights, MD 20740

International Standard Book Number
Paperbound: 978-0-7884-4404-3

Contents

Heritage Books by Michael Cecere:

A Brave, Active, and Intrepid Soldier:
Lieutenant Colonel Richard Campbell
of the Virginia Continental Line

A Good and Valuable Officer:
Daniel Morgan in the Revolutionary War

A Universal Appearance of War:
The Revolutionary War in Virginia, 1775–1781

An Officer of Very Extraordinary Merit:
Charles Porterfield and the American War for Independence, 1775–1780

Captain Thomas Posey and the 7th Virginia Regiment

Cast Off the British Yoke:
The Old Dominion and American Independence, 1763–1776

Great Things are Expected from the Virginians:
Virginia in the American Revolution

He Fell a Cheerful Sacrifice to His Country's Glorious Cause:
General William Woodford of Virginia, Revolutionary War Patriot

In This Time of Extreme Danger:
Northern Virginia in the American Revolution

Second to No Man but the Commander in Chief:
Hugh Mercer, American Patriot

They Are Indeed a Very Useful Corps:
American Riflemen in the Revolutionary War

They Behaved Like Soldiers:
Captain John Chilton and the Third Virginia Regiment, 1775–1778

To Hazard Our Own Security:
Maine's Role in the American Revolution

Virginia's Continentals, 1775–1778
Volume One

Virginia's Continentals, 1778–1783
Volume Two

Wedded to My Sword:
The Revolutionary War Service of Light Horse Harry Lee

Williamsburg at War:
Virginia's Colonial Capital in the Revolutionary War

Acknowledgements

This book is dedicated to my beloved dog, Sadie Belle, who so enjoyed our walks in Williamsburg.

This book was inspired by all the wonderful people at Colonial Williamsburg who have created and maintained a national treasure for generations to enjoy and appreciate.

I am particularly grateful to the staff at the Rockefeller Library at Colonial Williamsburg for maintaining an oasis of colonial knowledge within easy grasp of all visitors. I enjoy all my visits there and look forward to many more to come. The resources of the Jamestown-Yorktown Foundation were also helpful in the research of this book.

Lastly, I am very appreciative of the work that Debbie Riley, of Heritage Books, has done on this book as well as all my earlier books.

One

Road to War

On the eve of the Revolutionary War, Williamsburg, Virginia was a thriving colonial city of 1,900 inhabitants, roughly 900 who were white and free and the remaining 1,000 black and mostly enslaved.[1] Several hundred buildings, typically one and a half to two stories tall, some made of brick but most of wood, lined the city's main street, Duke of Gloucester, and its several side streets.[2]

With no significant manufacturing or deep-water port for trade, Williamsburg's economy centered largely on its role as the capital of Virginia. Hundreds of people travelled to Williamsburg regularly to conduct political, judicial, and commercial business and many of the city's residents made a living catering to these visitors. When Virginia's legislature, the House of Burgesses or the General Court were in session, the city's population swelled. Bi-annual meetings of merchants and planters who gathered in the shadow of the capitol to transact business, and those with business with the governor, whose residence was in the city, or with the county court of James City County, also generated commerce with their visits.

---

[1] Lorena S. Walsh, Ann Smart Martin, and Joanne Bowen, "Table 2.7: Population and Estimated Food Requirements in 1775," *Provisioning Early American Towns, The Chesapeake: A Multidisciplinary Case Study: Final Performance Report,* Colonial Williamsburg Foundation Library Research Report Series, No. 0404, 1997, 62.

[2] Department of Research, *General Description of Williamsburg: Compiled from Primary Source Material and Chronologically Arranged,* Department of Research and Record Colonial Williamsburg, 1942, 15, 17.

With so many people coming to, and staying in Williamsburg on a regular basis, it is not surprising that at least a dozen taverns, providing food, drink and lodging for the city's many guests, were in operation on the eve of the Revolutionary War.[3] The Raleigh and the King's Arms were popular establishments as were taverns operated by James Anderson (formerly Weatherburn's) and Christiana Campbell (located on the east side of the capitol building).

Filled with burgesses, planters, merchants and common folk from throughout Virginia and beyond, the taverns were convenient places to transact business and learn the latest news. The Raleigh Tavern stood out as the gathering place for Virginia's leaders who met there in 1769 and again in 1774 after royal governors dissolved the House of Burgesses. In each case the governor did so because of actions taken by the burgesses that he disapproved of. In 1769 it was their debate over the Townshend Duties and in 1774, the Intolerable Acts.

Within the Apollo room of the Raleigh Tavern gathered Peyton Randolph, Speaker of the House of Burgesses and Williamsburg's most prominent resident, Robert Carter Nicholas, the colonial treasurer and George Wythe, two other prominent city residents. They were joined by Patrick Henry, George Washington, Thomas Jefferson, Richard Henry Lee and many others to discuss and debate the issues they were not allowed to discuss in the House of Burgesses in 1769 and 1774.

While important political issues were debated in the Raleigh as well as the other taverns of Williamsburg, these public houses were also places for lodging, meals and entertainment. A French traveler to Virginia in 1765 recorded his impression of Williamsburg at a time when both the House

---

[3] James H. Soltow, *The Occupational Structure of Williamsburg in 1775,* Colonial Williamsburg Foundation Library Research Report Series 128, Colonial Williamsburg Foundation, 1990, 5-6.

of Burgesses was in session and scores of merchants had gathered to conduct business. Invited by several gentlemen to a tavern to spend an evening of gaming (gambling), an activity, observed the Frenchman, that was rampant in Williamsburg, he complained in his journal after the experience that,

> *Never was a more Disagreeable place than this at present. In the Daytime people hurrying back and forwards from the Capitol to the taverns, and at night, Carousing and Drinking in one Chamber, and box and Dice in another, which Continued till morning Commonly. There is not a publick house in Virginia but have their tables all battered with the boxes which shews the Extravagant Disposition of the planters.*[4]

Apparently, not every guest appreciated the entertaining nature of Williamsburg's taverns.

Although politics and the law were the primary drivers of Williamsburg's economy, its location between two prosperous counties, York and James City County, and two important rivers, the York and James, made it a convenient place for artisans and merchants to conduct business with nearby inhabitants and overnight travelers. In 1775, twenty-seven store keepers and merchants, six apothecaries, six tailors, six milliners, six wigmakers, barbers and hair dressers and three shoemakers made a living in the city.[5] Several carpenters, contractors, cabinet-makers, saddlers, coach makers and wheelwrights also operated businesses in Williamsburg as did

---

[4] *Journal of a French Traveler in the Colonies,* [New York 1921], 741-743 Pdf.https//www.loc.gov/item/ca33000046/.

[5] Soltow, *The Occupational Structure of Williamsburg in 1775,* Colonial Williamsburg Foundation Library Research Report Series 128, Colonial Williamsburg Foundation, 1990, 5-6.

several silversmiths and jewelers, two blacksmiths and a gunsmith.[6] It was these inhabitants of Williamsburg, along with their families and servants and slaves that made up the bulk of the population of the city. Some of these tradesmen even served in the governance of Williamsburg through the Common Hall, a sort of unelected city council formed when the city was chartered in 1722.

The Common Hall : Williamsburg's Governing Body

Williamsburg's Common Hall consisted of a mayor, a recorder (clerk/lawyer), six aldermen and twelve common councilors. The original members of the Common Hall were appointed by the King and served for life during good behavior. When a member of the Common Hall died or resigned, (either alderman or councilor) the vacancy was filled by the aldermen. The city mayor was elected annually by the Common Hall from among the aldermen.

Although there was little that was democratic about the selection of Common Hall members, the urban population from which they were drawn meant that the members of the Common Hall were more economically diverse than that of the House of Burgesses (which was dominated by Virginia planters). Several members of the Common Hall were skilled artisans and others were merchants, while a few doctors and lawyers were also members.[7]

On the eve of the Revolutionary War in 1775, the mayor of Williamsburg was John Dixon, printer and publisher of one of

---

[6] Ibid.

[7] Note: According to the 1722 Charter that established the Common Hall, its members were to meet on St. Andrews day to elect a mayor and fill any vacancies in the Common Hall. A survey of the Virginia Gazettes for the first week of December from 1766 to 1776 produced the list of counselors, aldermen, and mayor for 1775.

the three Virginia gazettes that was published in the capital every week. City aldermen in 1775 included Attorney General John Randolph, Thomas Everard, a lawyer and court clerk for the county of York, John Blair Jr., another lawyer, James Cocke, a prominent merchant, Dr. James Blair and Dr. William Pasteur, both physicians.[8]

Some of the members of the Common Council in 1775 included John Tazewell, a lawyer, James Geddy, a silversmith, Alexander Craig, a saddler, Benjamin Powell, an undertaker (building contractor) and Robert Miller, a merchant. Several other counselors remain unidentified.[9] All of these men formed the Common Hall, which was charged with addressing the local concerns and problems of the city's residents.

Virginia's Leaders on the Eve of War

As the seat of government for the colony of Virginia, Williamsburg was also the residence of some of the colony's most important political leaders. On the eve of the Revolutionary War this included the royal governor, **John Murray, the 4th Earl of Dunmore**. Lord Dunmore, who reluctantly relinquished the post of governor in New York to assume the post in Virginia in 1771, was a Scotsman with a fiery temper. Destined to be the last royal governor of Virginia, he was joined in Williamsburg in February 1774 by his wife Charlotte and six of their seven children (their youngest son remained in Scotland). While Dunmore's official residence, the Governor's Palace located at the end of Palace Street, may not have matched the standards that Lord Dunmore and his family were accustomed to in Scotland, it was arguably the

---

[8] Note: A survey of the Virginia Gazettes for the first week of December from 1766 to 1776 produced the list of counselors, aldermen, and mayor for 1775.

[9] Ibid.

most elegant house in Williamsburg, if not all of Virginia, and dozens of servants (some paid and others indentured) as well as a great number of slaves worked hard to serve the Governor and his family's every need.[10]

While Lord Dunmore represented the chief executive authority in the colony (in the name of King George III) the leading legislative figure in Virginia was the Speaker of the House of Burgesses, **Peyton Randolph**. Speaker Randolph lived with his wife, Elizabeth, and numerous household slaves on Nicholson Street, within a short walk of the Governor's Palace and an even shorter walk from the county courthouse and market square, which were situated directly across from Randolph's house in the center of Williamsburg. Trained in the law in London, Peyton Randolph devoted most of his adult life to public service, first as Attorney General and then as Speaker of the House of Burgesses (representing the city of Williamsburg in the assembly). The high regard in which Speaker Randolph was held among all Virginians was shared by the delegates assembled in Philadelphia at the First Continental Congress in 1774. Randolph was selected by these men to preside over the Congress in September of 1774 and again in May of 1775 at the Second Continental Congress.[11]

John Randolph, the Attorney General of Virginia, was Peyton Randolph's younger brother. He too lived near market square, within view of the courthouse, but on the opposite side on what is now South England Street. He followed a similar path to his brother, studying law in London and becoming the Clerk to the House of Burgesses in 1752. John Randolph replaced his brother as Attorney General upon Peyton's

---

[10] John E. Selby, *Dunmore,* Virginia Independence Bicentennial Commission, 1977, 10-19.

[11] Inventory and Appraisement of the Estate of Peyton Randolph Esq. in York County taken January 5th, 1776.

selection as Speaker of the House of Burgesses in 1766. He also served in the House of Burgesses as the College of William and Mary's representative and was an alderman for the city of Williamsburg. Although Peyton and John Randolph shared a strong commitment to public service, their views diverged significantly regarding the growing political dispute with the British parliament. Unlike his brother Peyton, who was politically moderate in his opposition to Parliament, John Randolph argued forcefully against actions by the colonists that challenged parliamentary authority. He viewed the First Virginia Convention and the First Continental Congress, both held in 1774, as extra-legal and thus illegal assemblies and he urged Virginians to refrain from disloyal actions that provoked Parliament and the King.[12]

Robert Carter Nicholas, the Treasurer of Virginia, was viewed by all who knew him as a pious, even tempered man. On the eve of the Revolution, Nicholas lived on Francis Street, across from the powder magazine and courthouse, with his wife and ten children. Nicholas had attended William and Mary and possessed land outside of Williamsburg from which he derived a generous income. He was elected to the House of Burgesses in 1756 as a representative from York County (living at the time in a house adjacent to the Governor's Palace). In 1761, Nicholas gave up his seat in the assembly and relocated to Francis Street, which was situated in James City County. He returned to the House of Burgesses in 1766 as a representative from James City County and was appointed that same year as treasurer of the colony at the death of the former treasurer and Speaker of the House of Burgesses, John Robinson. It was as

[12] William J. Van Schreeven and Robert L. Scribner, eds., *Revolutionary Virginia: The Road to Independence,* Vol. 1, (University Press of Virginia, 1973), 204-205.

treasurer that Robert Carter Nicholas served Virginia during the Revolution.[13]

George Wythe, a lawyer who many in Virginia believed possessed one of the colony's best legal minds, resided in a grand brick building on the palace green within sight of the Governor's Palace. When he was not tutoring the likes of Thomas Jefferson in the law or arguing cases before the General Court, Wythe served his fellow citizens of Williamsburg as a city alderman and mayor, responsibilities he surrendered in 1773 upon his resignation as an alderman. Like the Randolphs and Robert Carter Nicholas, Wythe also held an important post in the colonial government in 1775, he served as Clerk of the House of Burgesses. In this position, Wythe assisted burgesses with their bills and resolutions, something his keen legal mind was well suited for. Wythe served as a burgess himself during the early years of the dispute with Parliament and was well versed on the troubles. His experience and vast legal knowledge led to his selection as a delegate to the Continental Congress in 1776. Among Virginia's signers of the Declaration of Independence, George Wythe's name comes first, a testament to the high regard his fellow Virginians had for him.[14]

These five men (Lord Dunmore, Peyton Randolph, John Randolph, Robert Carter Nicholas, and George Wythe) held the principle government posts in Virginia in 1775 and wielded great influence in the governance of the colony. They were frequently joined in Williamsburg by such notable figures as Patrick Henry, George Washington, Thomas Jefferson, Richard Henry Lee, and many other burgesses who represented the

---

[13] William J. Van Schreeven and Robert L. Scribner, eds., "Footnote 2," *Revolutionary Virginia: The Road to Independence,* Vol. 2, (University Press of Virginia, 1975), 11-12.

[14] Robert L. Scribner, ed., "Footnote 11," *Revolutionary Virginia: The Road to Independence* Vol. 3, (University Press of Virginia, 1977), 423-424.

freeholders of Virginia's various counties in the House of Burgesses.

Williamsburg: Hotbed of Opposition to Parliament

As Williamsburg was the political, legal, and commercial hub of Virginia, it was only natural that opposition in Virginia to the efforts of British authorities to exert greater control over the colonies was centered in the capital city. Patrick Henry's 1765 Stamp Act Resolves, which were narrowly supported by the House of Burgesses, rallied colonists throughout British America to oppose the Stamp Act. Opposition to the Stamp Act in Williamsburg nearly turned violent on the eve of its implementation in the fall of 1765 when a large, angry crowd confronted James Mercer, the appointed stamp tax collector, near the capitol. Threatened with bodily injury, Mercer was rescued from the hostile crowd by the royal governor, Francis Fauquier, who witnessed the confrontation from the porch of Charlton's coffeehouse and intervened on Mercer's behalf. At this early stage of the dispute, few Virginians dared to confront Governor Fauquier, the King's representative in Virginia. As for Mercer, he promptly resigned as Virginia's stamp tax collector the next day, delaying the implementation of the tax.[15]

The repeal of the Stamp Act in 1766 temporarily decreased tension in the colonies, but concern and anger returned in 1768 with Parliament's adoption of the Townshend Duties. The House of Burgesses demonstrated its opposition to these duties in the spring of 1769 with a series of resolves, but the assembly was dissolved by the new royal governor, Lord Botetourt, before the resolves were passed. Botetourt viewed the burgesses' actions as insulting to the British crown.

---

[15] Joseph Royal, "October 25, 1765," *Virginia Gazette, Supplement*, 3.

Undeterred by Botetourt's decision, most of the dismissed burgesses gathered in the Apollo room of Anthony Hay's Raleigh Tavern to discuss the situation and consider a non-importation plan introduced by Colonel George Washington of Fairfax County on behalf of his absent friend and neighbor, Colonel George Mason. The plan sought to prohibit the importation of a list of British goods through a voluntary non-importation association [boycott].[16] It was adopted by those in attendance at the Raleigh and soon spread throughout Virginia. Similar versions of the boycott were adopted in the other American colonies and although it was not universally implemented or enforced, the reduction in trade did likely influence Parliament's decision to repeal most of the Townshend duties in 1770.

Although several years of relative calm settled over the colonies, many remained distrustful of the British Parliament and Ministry. The desire and need for colonial unity led to the formation of committees of correspondence in the colonies in 1773. The period of calm that settled over Virginia following the repeal of the Townshend Duties was disturbed once again in May 1774 when news of Parliament's reaction to the Boston Tea Party arrived.

Opposition to Parliament Grows : 1774

Although many Virginians disapproved of the destruction of tea in Boston in late 1773 [the Tea Party], Parliament's harsh crack down on Massachusetts shocked most Virginians. The House of Burgesses responded by calling for a day of fasting and prayer in Virginia on June 1, 1774, the day Parliament's Boston Port bill took effect. The action of the House of

---

[16] Van Schreeven and Scribner, eds., "Non-Importation Resolutions of the Former Burgesses, May 18, 1769," *Revolutionary Virginia: The Road to Independence,* Vol. 1, 72-77.

Burgesses angered the royal governor, Lord Dunmore, who believed the resolution insulted Parliament and the King, so he dissolved the House of Burgesses in response.

Like they had in 1769, many of the dismissed burgesses gathered in the Apollo room of the Raleigh Tavern, now owned by James Southall, to discuss how they should respond. On May 27, eighty-nine members declared that Parliament's actions against Massachusetts were not only a grievous violation of the British constitution, but a systematic effort to reduce all the American colonists to a state of slavery.[17] The former burgesses accused the East India Company of colluding with Parliament to deprive the colonies of their rights. They pledged to boycott all the company's goods, except spices and saltpeter, until the acts against Massachusetts were repealed.[18] They also called for a general meeting of the colonies to foster greater unity among them.

Satisfied with these measures, most of the dismissed burgesses left the capital the next day to return to their homes. A few were still in Williamsburg when Peyton Randolph received word from the north on May 29, that leaders from New England and the mid-Atlantic colonies had proposed a boycott of all British goods and a general congress in Philadelphia to discuss the crisis. Randolph summoned the representatives that were still in Williamsburg to discuss the news and twenty-five of them met, once again, in the Apollo Room of the Raleigh on May 30, where they decided that a colony wide convention was needed to select and instruct Virginia's delegation to the

---

[17] Van Schreeven and Scribner, eds., "An Association Signed by 89 Members of the late House of Burgesses, May 27, 1774," *Revolutionary Virginia: The Road to Independence,* Vol. 1, 97-98.
[18] Ibid.

Philadelphia Congress.[19] Dispatches were sent to summon county representatives to meet in Williamsburg in early August.

The citizens of Williamsburg gathered at the courthouse on the afternoon of May 30, to learn of the decisions made at the Raleigh Tavern and they unanimously approved the measures.[20] Two days later, on June 1, the inhabitants of Williamsburg gathered again at the courthouse and, led by Speaker Randolph and the city's other prominent leaders, marched in procession to Bruton Church to pray for and demonstrate their support for the people of Boston and Massachusetts.[21]

The news from New England grew bleaker as the summer progressed and thousands of British troops arrived in Boston to enforce the harsh measures of Parliament, measures the colonists dubbed, the Intolerable Acts.

Governor Dunmore's dismissal of the House of Burgesses in late May before the assembly had completed its business and renewed the expired court fees law meant that legal proceedings for civil cases such as debt collection and the recording of wills and deeds were suspended until a new law was approved. Another expired law that needed to be renewed was the militia law. Without it, county officials had little authority to call out or train the militia.

The dissolution of the assembly meant that new elections were necessary, so Governor Dunmore issued writs (orders) in mid-June, but three weeks later he unexpectedly left Williamsburg to lead a military expedition against the Shawnee Indians in the western part of the colony.[22] Although his absence from the capital, which lasted until December, meant that no new laws were possible, it allowed the First Virginia

---

[19] Ibid, 99-100.

[20] Purdie & Dixon, "June 2, 1774," *Virginia Gazette*, 2.

[21] Ibid.

[22] Purdie & Dixon, "July 14, 1774," *Virginia Gazette*, 2.

Convention to convene in Williamsburg in early August without fear of interference from the governor.

First Virginia Convention

A few days after Dunmore's departure, the freeholders of Williamsburg gathered again at the courthouse and unanimously elected Peyton Randolph to represent them in both the upcoming convention and the House of Burgesses (whenever it met again).[23] On August 1, county delegates (two per county) met in convention in the capitol in Williamsburg to select representatives for the upcoming Continental Congress in Philadelphia and draft instructions for them. Many of the convention delegates arrived with instructions for bold action from their county committees. They selected Peyton Randolph, George Washington, Patrick Henry, Richard Henry Lee, Edmund Pendleton, Benjamin Harrison, and Richard Bland as representatives to the general Congress in Philadelphia. The Convention then instructed the delegation to simultaneously reaffirm Virginia's desire for close ties with Britain and defend the colonists' constitutional rights.

The Virginia Convention gave Parliament until November 1, 1774, to repeal its acts against Massachusetts or face a general boycott. Other provisions called for a ban on the further importation of slaves and a ban on the consumption of tea. The Convention even went as far as to authorize a ban on colonial exports to Britain in September 1775 if Parliament remained intransigent with its policies.[24]

With Virginia's representatives to the Congress selected and their instructions drafted, the convention adjourned on August 6. Peyton Randolph met with the inhabitants of

---

[23] Ibid.
[24] Ibid.

Williamsburg on August 10, at the courthouse where those assembled, "*generally approved of the Association*" adopted by the convention. Contributions in cash and provisions were also raised for thc relief of Boston.[25]

Independent Militia Companies Form

Although economic measures to oppose the British ministry's actions against Boston were the preferred option of nearly all Virginians, one county in northern Virginia boldly embraced more aggressive measures. Like their fellow Virginians, the freeholders of Fairfax County initially approved economic sanctions against Britain at their committee meeting in July. However, in the weeks following this decision, distressing reports of British military activity in Massachusetts caused many to question whether economic sanctions went far enough to oppose Parliament.[26]

Prompted by these alarming reports, writers to the Virginia gazettes boldly proclaimed in late July the willingness of Virginians to fight for their constitutional rights. "*Do they think we will submit to Tyranny in our own Land*?" asked one writer. "*The Country which our Fathers purchased with their Blood, we will defend with our Blood.*"[27] This view was echoed a week later by a self described American Cato who reminded readers that, "*With the Sword our Forefathers obtained their constitutional Rights, and by the Sword it is our Duty to defend them.*"[28]

It was in this tense atmosphere that the leaders and freeholders of Fairfax County gathered in late September to debate a new measure drafted by Colonel George Mason. Laws

---

[25] Purdie & Dixon, "August 11, 1774," *Virginia Gazette*, 3.
[26] Purdie & Dixon, "July 21, 1774," *Virginia Gazette*, 1.
[27] Ibid.
[28] Purdie and Dixon, "July 28, 1774," *Virginia Gazette*, 1.

for the regulation of the militia in Virginia dated back to 1738 and were periodically amended in the years leading up to 1774 with temporary acts of the assembly, (most recently in 1771) but when Governor Dunmore suddenly dissolved the House of Burgesses in May 1774 he denied the assembly the chance to renew the expired 1771 militia law.

What should have happened next was that Virginia's militia laws reverted back to acts passed in 1738, but confusion and disagreement on this paralyzed Virginia's leaders. Many were uncertain as to whether they still had the authority to assemble the militia and the result, according to an inquiry by the House of Burgesses into the causes of the unhappy disturbances of 1774-75 was, "*an almost total inattention to the proper training and disciplining of our Militia.*"[29] The cancellation of these musters was likely welcomed by many Virginians (who tended to dislike militia service anyway) but those cognizant of the threat Britain now posed to the colonies were alarmed. The gentlemen and freeholders of Fairfax County responded first, proclaiming on September 21, that,

> *In this Time of extreme Danger, with the Indian Enemy in our Country, and threat'ned with the Destruction of our Civil-rights, & Liberty, and all that is dear to British Subjects & Freemen; we the Subscribers, taking into our serious consideration the present alarming Situation of all the British Colonies upon this Continent as well as our own, being sensible of the Expediency of putting the Militia of this Colony upon a more respectable Footing, & hoping to excite others by our Example, have voluntarily freely & cordially*

---

[29] John Pendleton Kennedy, ed., "Address of the House of Burgesses to Governor Dunmore, June 19, 1775," *Journal of the House of Burgesses: 1773-1776*, (Richmond: VA, 1905), 256.

> *entered into the following Association.... That we will form ourselves into a Company, not exceeding one hundred Men, by the Name of The Fairfax independent Company of Voluntiers....*[30]

The Fairfax Independent Company of Volunteers was not formed to replace the temporarily defunct county militia, but rather, to serve as a training vehicle in which future militia officers learned the military arts. Neighboring Prince William County followed Fairfax in November with their own independent militia company and Loudoun and Spotsylvania counties did likewise in December.

Nicholas Cresswell, a British loyalist who had recently arrived in Virginia, observed the heightened militancy in the colony in the fall of 1774 and noted in his diary in October that:

> *Everything here is in the utmost confusion. Committees are appointed to inspect into the Characters and Conduct of every tradesman, to prevent them selling Tea or buying British Manufactures. Some of them have been tarred and feathered, others had their property burnt and destroyed by the populace. Independent Companies are raising in every County on the Continent...and train their Men as if they were on the Eve of War...*[Contributions are raised] *in every Colony on the Continent for the relief of the people of Boston. The King is openly cursed, and his authority set at defiance. In short, everything is ripe for rebellion. The New Englanders by their canting, whining, insinuating tricks have persuaded the rest of the*

[30] Robert A. Rutland, ed., "Fairfax County Militia Association September 21, 1774," *The Papers of George Mason*, Vol. 1, (Chapel Hill: University of North Carolina Press, 1970), 210-211.

Colonies that the Government is going to make absolute slaves of them.[31]

Although Cresswell's claim that independent companies were forming all over the continent was exaggerated, his observations of Virginia in late October 1774 certainly attested to the lengths many Virginians were willing to go to resist Parliament.

Williamsburg Independent Militia Company

It appears that at some point in the fall of 1774, "*several young Gentlemen and others*" of Williamsburg, totaling approximately 50 men, formed themselves into an independent militia company with the express intent to learn the military exercise.[32] While it is unclear exactly when this militia company was formed, its commander, John Dixon, (an alderman) noted the existence of an independent militia company in Norfolk that was formed several years earlier as justification for the Williamsburg company.[33] The members of the company selected Dixon as their captain and mustered once a week to improve their military skills.[34] This was a significant increase in training compared to the regular county militia, which typically mustered once every three months for company drill. At some point in the fall, while Lord Dunmore was still away on the frontier, John Blair Sr., the President of the governor's privy council, "*directed the keeper of the Public*

---

[31] Nicholas Cresswell, "October 24, 1774," *The Journal of Nicholas Cresswell*, (The Dial Press: NY, 1974), 43-44.

[32] Kennedy, ed., "Testimony of John Frederick Miller and Benjamin Waller," *Journal of the House of Burgesses*: 1773-1776, 223, 232.

[33] Kennedy, ed. "Testimony of John Dixon," *Journal of the House of Burgesses*: *1773-1776*, 233.

[34] Kennedy, ed. "Testimony of Benjamin Waller and the Testimony of John Dixon," *Journal of the House of Burgesses*: *1773-1776,* 232-33.

Magazine, to furnish the Company with Muskets."[35] The independent company welcomed Governor Dunmore back to Williamsburg upon his return in early December. John Dixon described the occasion.

> *One of the Company waited upon his Excellency to inform him the Company intended to pay their Compliments to him the next Morning before the Palace, if agreeable to Lady Dunmore, who was then indisposed* [recovering from childbirth], *but his Lordship being out of the way, the person who went left his Compliments of the above import. The next Morning* [Captain Dixon] *with part of the Company, drew up in Palace Street and paid the usual Compliments. His Lordship did not come out to meet them, but some time afterwords there was a Message delivered by Mr. Blair from his Excellency, that he would have done himself the pleasure of waiting upon them if they had staid a little longer, as he did not expect that they would have finished their Exercise so soon.*[36]

Benjamin Waller, who apparently heard of the affair second hand, described it a bit differently.

> *When his Excellency returned from the Indian Expedition last fall many of the said Company waited upon him in their uniform to congratulate his Lordship on his Return, but…they were cooly received.*[37]

---

[35] Kennedy, ed. "Testimony of John Dixon," *Journal of the House of Burgesses: 1773-1776*, 232-33.
[36] Ibid.
[37] Kennedy, ed. "Testimony of Benjamin Waller," *Journal of the House of Burgesses: 1773-1776*, 232.

Although Lord Dunmore never commented on his reaction to the reception of the Williamsburg Independent Company, he did inform his superior in England, Lord Dartmouth, in a long dispatch on the events in Virginia, about the existence of both the independent militia companies and the county committees that had formed in almost every jurisdiction to enforce Congress's non-importation resolutions. Dunmore accurately characterized the purpose and activity of the committees, but he significantly exaggerated the number of independent militia companies that had formed.

> *Every county besides is now arming a company of men whom they call an independent company for the avowed purpose of protecting their* [county] *committees and to be employed against government if occasion require.*[38]

Williamsburg Committee

The inhabitants of Williamsburg formed their committee to enforce Congress's Non-Importation Association on December 22, well after the independent militia company had formed. Committee members included:

Peyton Randolph	Speaker of the House of Burgesses
Robert Carter Nicholas	Treasurer for the colony
George Wythe	Clerk of the House of Burgesses
John Dixon	Alderman, Mayor, and Printer
Benjamin Waller	City Recorder and Attorney
Thomas Everard	Alderman and York County Clerk
James Cocke	Alderman and Merchant

---

[38] K.G. Davies, ed. "Lord Dunmore to Lord Dartmouth, December 24, 1774," *Documents of the American Revolution: 1770-1783,* Vo. 8, (Irish University Press, 1975), 266.

William Pasteur	Alderman and Physician
Benjamin Powell	Councilor and General Contractor
John Tazewell	Councilor and Lawyer
James Southall	Tavern Keeper
James Hubard	Merchant
Robert Nicholson	Merchant
John Carter	Merchant
Dr. John M. Galt	Physician[39]

Tension Mounts: 1774-75

While county committees throughout Virginia met in December to oversee enforcement of Congress's non-importation agreement, more disturbing reports from England appeared in the newspapers. Britain had halted all gunpowder and arms shipments to the colonies.[40] If the reports were true, it meant that British officials were worried about increased colonial opposition and possibly violence and their solution was to deny the colonists the means to resist.

Along with the troubling news about the gunpowder and arms restrictions, the gazettes were also filled with reports of ever more British reinforcements sailing to the colonies, specifically two regiments for New York and hundreds of Marines with a second naval fleet to Boston.[41] These reports suggested to a growing number of Virginians (and their fellow American colonists) that the British Ministry was preparing to use armed force to exert its will.

Williamsburg's leaders undoubtedly paid close attention to these reports and did their best to enforce the non-importation association, advertising the sale at auction of several packages imported from European that were voluntarily surrendered to

[39] Purdie and Dixon, "December 22, 1774," *Virginia Gazette*, 3.
[40] Dixon and Hunter, "December 8, 1774," *Virginia Gazette, Supplement*, 2.
[41] Ibid.

the committee in mid-January and again in February.[42] The owners of these goods, per article 10 of Congress's non-importation agreement, were to be reimbursed for their costs, and whatever profits were derived from the auction was to go towards the relief of Boston.

1775

Not all the focus of Williamsburg that winter was directed on the political dispute with Parliament. Like their fellow Virginians to the west, the inhabitants of Williamsburg welcomed news of Lord Dunmore's successful expedition against the Shawnee Indians in the fall of 1774. Upon his return in December, the Common Hall of the city submitted an address congratulating Dunmore on both his success in the west and the birth of a daughter. The Governor and his wife endeared themselves to many Virginians by naming their newborn daughter, Virginia. In mid-January, Governor Dunmore held a "*ball and elegant entertainment...attended by a numerous company of Ladies and Gentlemen*," to celebrate the birth of his daughter.[43] The affair provided a pleasant distraction for many in Williamsburg, but only temporarily for the crisis with Britain remained.

Confirmation of the King's ban on gunpowder and arms exports to America (which came in the form of a circular letter from Lord Dartmouth to the various colonial governors that found its way into the newspapers) prompted more county committees into action.[44] Dunmore County (in the northwest region of Virginia) made arrangements to purchase and store all of the gunpowder in the possession of local merchants while

---

[42] Dixon and Hunter, "January 21, 1775," and "February 4, 1775," *Virginia Gazette*, 3.
[43] Dixon and Hunter, "January 21, 1775," *Virginia Gazette*, 2.
[44] Dixon & Hunter, "January 14, 1775," *Virginia Gazette,* 1.

Northampton County (on the eastern shore) offered a reward to the first person in the county who could manufacture 500 pounds of gunpowder.[45] Caroline and Cumberland counties also took measures to secure gunpowder, while Isle of Wight and Fauquier County moved to form their own independent militia companies.[46]

For every county that took these aggressive measures, however, another clung to the hope that the economic sanctions adopted by the Continental Congress would succeed and make military preparations unnecessary. Such hope dimmed when the colonists learned that there had not been a groundswell of support for the colonists among the English electorate in recent parliamentary elections. Rather, most of the members of Parliament won reelection in England and it appeared that concern for the rights of the American colonists barely registered with the English electorate.[47]

Despite this demoralizing news, Virginia's leaders continued their opposition to Britain by calling for a second convention of county representatives to meet in March. With Lord Dunmore back in the capital it was thought best to hold the convention in Richmond. County committees held

---

[45] Van Schreeven and Scribner, ed., "Proceedings of Dunmore County Committee, January 10, 1775 and Northampton County Committee, January 11, 1775," *Revolutionary Virginia: The Road to Independence,* Vol. 2, 229, 231.

[46] Van Schreeven and Scribner, ed., "Proceedings of the Caroline County Committee, February 9 and March 8, 1775, Cumberland County Committee, February 18, 1775, and Isle of Wight Committee, February 13, 1775, *Revolutionary Virginia: The Road to Independence,* Vol. 2, 284, 317, 293, 286-287, and Beverly H. Runge, ed., "February 16, 1775," *The Papers of George Washington, Colonial Series,* Vol. 10, (Charlottesville and London: University Press of Virginia, 1995), 263-64.

[47] Lewis Namier and John Brooks, *The History of Parliament: The House of Commons, 1754-1790*, (Online) https://www.historyofparliamentonline.org/volume/1754-1790/survey/iii-members.

meetings throughout the winter to select their delegates, and on February 3, the inhabitants of Williamsburg met at the courthouse to once again unanimously elect Peyton Randolph to represent them at the convention.[48]

Second Virginia Convention

The possibility of armed conflict with Great Britain weighed heavy on Patrick Henry and his fellow convention delegates as they gathered at what is now St. John's Church in Richmond in late March. They gathered to select representatives to the next Continental Congress (scheduled to meet in Philadelphia in May) and provide them with instructions. The most memorable development at the convention occurred on the fourth day when Patrick Henry proposed that Virginia, "*Be immediately put into a posture of defense*."[49] He firmly believed that armed conflict with Britain was inevitable and he urged his fellow delegates to place the colony on a war footing.

Henry's proposal was opposed by moderates like Edmund Pendleton and Robert Carter Nicholas. They argued that such a move was too confrontational and would provoke Parliament. They urged patience and scoffed at the idea of fighting Britain.[50]

Patrick Henry replied to his critics and in doing so delivered one of the most memorable phrases of the American Revolution. Many years later, William Wirt attempted to document and recreate Henry's famous speech at the Second

---

[48] Purdie, "February 3, 1775," *Virginia Gazette,* 2.

[49] Van Schreeven and Scribner, ed., "Proceedings of the 2nd Virginia Convention, March 23, 1775," *Revolutionary Virginia: The Road to Independence,* Vol. 2, 366-367.

[50] William Wirt, *Sketches in the Life and Character of Patrick Henry,* (Philadelphia, 1817), 136.

Convention in his biography of Patrick Henry. Through correspondence and interviews with the few people who were still alive forty years after the speech, Wirt re-created Henry's speech (which was delivered extemporaneously in 1775). With the passage of so much time, the accuracy of its wording is certainly questionable, but Wirt likely captured the spirit of Henry's speech.

Patrick Henry began with an acknowledgement of the patriotism of those who opposed him, but suggested that they had, "*shut* [their] *eyes against a painful truth.*"[51] Henry was alarmed by Britain's military buildup in Massachusetts and asked the delegates a pointed question:

> *Are fleets and armies necessary*…[for] *reconciliation? Have we shown ourselves so unwilling to be reconciled, that force must be called in to win back our love? Let us not deceive ourselves, sir. These are the implements of war and subjugation—the last arguments to which kings resort…I ask gentlemen, sir, what means this martial array, if its purpose be not to force us to submission…Has Great Britain any enemy in this quarter of the world, to call for all this accumulation of navies and armies? No, sir, she has none. They are meant for us, they can be meant for no other. They are sent over to bind and rivet upon us those chains which the British ministry have been so long forging….*[52]

Henry then recounted the failure of the numerous pleas and petitions sent to Britain over the past decade:

---

[51] Ibid, 138.
[52] Ibid, 139.

> *In vain, after these* [appeals and petitions] *may we indulge the fond hope of peace and reconciliation. There is no longer any room for hope. If we wish to be free…we must fight! I repeat it, sir, we must fight!*[53]

Henry confidently exclaimed that, "*Three million people, armed in the holy cause of liberty…are invincible by any force which our enemy can send against us.*"[54] He then asserted that conflict was inevitable and urged the delegates to prepare the colony for it. He closed with his famous phrase, "*I know not what course others may take, but as for me, Give Me Liberty or Give Me Death!*"[55]

Henry's stirring appeal worked, and his resolution passed by a narrow margin. A committee was formed to, "*prepare a Plan for embodying, arming and disciplining such a Number of Men,*" as was sufficient to put the colony into a posture of defense.[56] The committee, made up of Patrick Henry, George Washington, Richard Henry Lee, Thomas Jefferson, and Edmund Pendleton, drafted a plan by the next day and it was adopted by the Convention a day after that. It began by recommending that the colony diligently put into execution the Militia Law of 1738, which the committee claimed, "has become in force by the expiration of all subsequent militia laws."[57]

---

[53] Ibid, 140.
[54] Ibid, 141.
[55] Ibid.
[56] Van Schreeven and Scribner, ed., "Proceedings of the 2nd Virginia Convention, March 23, 1775," *Revolutionary Virginia: The Road to Independence,* Vol. 2, 366-367.
[57] Van Schreeven and Scribner, ed., "Proceedings of the 2nd Virginia Convention, March 25, 1775," *Revolutionary Virginia: The Road to Independence,* Vol. 2, 374.

To address the immediate weakness of the colony's militia forces and bridge the gap until the 1738 militia law could be fully implemented, the Convention,

> *Recommended to the Inhabitants of the several Counties of this Colony that they form one or more volunteer Companies of Infantry and Troops of Horse in each County and be in constant training and Readiness to act on any Emergency.*[58]

The plan identified counties that should raise cavalry and those better served to raise companies of infantry. Williamsburg was urged to raise both.[59] Hunting shirts, a sort of course linen frock, were the recommended uniform for all of the troops and the plan specified the number of officers and rank and file for each company along with their arms, gear, and even the military drill they were to use, his Majesty's 1764 drill.[60] The plan also recommended that all of the county committees collect funds from their constituents to supply their militia companies with an adequate supply of ammunition and arms.[61]

The fact that the Convention recommended instead of required these measures suggests that the delegates recognized their own legal limitations as an extra-legal assembly. No provision was made to enforce these measures if a county refused to adopt them; such an unpleasant possibility was ignored because the Convention recognized the questionable legality of the measures.

Non-compliance with the Convention's requests was never seriously considered in Williamsburg. Led by James Innes, the head usher at the grammar school of William and Mary, and

---

[58] Ibid, 375.
[59] Ibid.
[60] Ibid.
[61] Ibid.

George Nicholas, the eldest son of Virginia's treasurer, Robert Carter Nicholas, a volunteer company of militia was formed in April in Williamsburg per the Second Virginia Convention's instructions.[62] It appears this volunteer company replaced (or perhaps absorbed) the independent company that had been formed in 1774.[63] John Dixon, the original commander of the independent company, had either stepped aside (perhaps as a result of his election as mayor of Williamsburg) or been replaced by Innes. It is safe to assume, however, that many of the members of Williamsburg's independent company of 1774 also served in Captain Innes's company of volunteers in 1775.[64]

---

[62] Lyon G. Tyler, ed., "The Williamsburg Companies," *Tyler's Quarterly Historical and Genealogical Magazine*, Vol. 9, (Richmond, VA, 1928), 46-47.

Note: James Innes is identified as the captain of the Volunteer Company of the City of Williamsburg in a June 6, 1775 entry in the Journals of the House of Burgesses. See: Kennedy, ed. "June 6, 1775," *Journal of the House of Burgesses*: 1773-1776, 198.

[63] Kennedy, ed. "Testimony of John Randolph," *Journal of the House of Burgesses*: 1773-1776, 232.

Note: Attorney General John Randolph, in a deposition concerning an incident at the Williamsburg gunpowder magazine in late April 1775, recalled that "*he does not recollect he ever saw any of the People under Arms, (except on the Removal of the Powder) but the volunteer Company, when exercising, which Company had been formed a considerable time before the disturbance happened.*" Unfortunately, it is unclear what Randolph considers a "considerable time" so it is possible he viewed the independent company of 1774 and the new volunteer company of 1775 as one and the same.

[64] Note: Several references in Pinkney's Virginia Gazette to "the volunteer company" suggests that only one such company of volunteers existed in Williamsburg in the spring of 1775. (See: Pinkney's Virginia Gazette, May 11 and June 8, 1775.) John Greenhow recalled many years later, however, that, "*the youth of Williamsburg, among whom he was one formed themselves into a military corps and chose Henry Nicholson for their captain.*" (See: Tyler, ed., "The Williamsburg Companies," *Tyler's Quarterly Historical and Genealogical Magazine*, Vol. 9, 46-47). This company of youths was not an actual military unit as called for by the 2nd Virginia Convention.

It does not appear that a troop of horse, (consisting of thirty horsemen plus officers) was formed in Williamsburg in 1775.

Two

Spring and Summer of 1775

Many of the residents of Williamsburg learned of the actions of the Second Virginia Convention in Richmond through their local gazettes. John Pinkney's newspaper was the first to publish the proceedings of the convention on March 30, followed two days later by the gazette published by John Dixon and William Hunter.[1] It is unclear how long it took James Innes and George Nicholas to implement (or if the volunteer company was already formed, incorporate) the recommendations of the Convention, but based on reports in the newspapers, there was an urgency to do so.

In the several months leading up to the convention in Richmond, letters from England and the other colonies printed in the newspapers left readers uncertain of what to expect. Some of the published letters claimed that the British parliament was wavering in its stance towards the colonies and the British people (particularly the merchants and even the King) were on the colonists' side. Other reports, however, emphasized Parliament's determination to hold firm and punish the American colonists.

Hope for reconciliation dimmed considerably in the spring with a steady stream of correspondence from England announcing that, "*all hopes of an accommodation were at an*

---

[1] John Pinkney, "Proceedings of the Second Virginia Convention, March 30, 1775," *Virginia Gazette,* 2-3 and John Dixon and William Hunter, "Proceedings of the Second Virginia Convention, April 1, 1775, *Virginia Gazette,* 2-3.

end."[2] The news grew worse by mid-April with further reports that, "*It is a determined point* [of Parliament] *not to repeal any of the acts against America, but to proceed to vigorous measures*," and "*Great preparations are making by the Ministry, to reduce the Americans to obedience*."[3] Such disturbing statements undoubtedly increased the anxiety of those who read them. To make matters worse, an alarming rumor circulated through Williamsburg in mid-April that Governor Dunmore intended to seize the gunpowder and weapons stored in the powder magazine in the center of the city. Edmund Pendleton, a prominent member of the House of Burgesses from Caroline County, some eighty miles from Williamsburg, heard whispers to this effect and commented about the matter to Colonel George Washington on April 21.

> *We have a loose Report that the Govr. has taken the Key of the Magazine, & that a sloop with a Company of Marines was lying in each of the Creeks, which it was Supposed were to take the Arms & Ammunition from thence.*[4]

Mr. Pendleton had no idea how accurate his suspicion was. Just hours before he wrote to Colonel Washington, twenty British marines and sailors from the HMS *Magdalen* landed at Burwell's Ferry on the James River and rapidly marched to

---

[2] Alexander Purdie, "March 31, 1775," *Virginia Gazette Supplement*, 1.

[3] Pinkney, "April 13, 1775," *Virginia Gazette*, 2 and Purdie, "April 14, 1775," *Virginia Gazette*, 2.

[4] W.W. Abbot and Dorothy Twohig, eds. "Edmund Pendleton to George Washington, April 21, 1775," *The Papers of George Washington*, Vol. 10, (Charlottesville, VA: University Press of Virginia, 1995), 340.

Williamsburg, four miles away.[5] Just as Pendleton and many others feared, their orders, at the behest of Governor Dunmore, were to seize the gunpowder stored in the powder magazine and transport it back to their ship. Lord Dunmore explained the rationale behind this provocative act in a letter to his superiors in England:

> *The series of dangerous measures pursued by the people of this colony against government, which they have now entirely overturned and particularly their having come to a resolution of raising a body of armed men in all of the counties, made me think it prudent to remove some gunpowder which was in a magazine in this place where it lay exposed to any attempt that might be made to seize it, and I had reason to believe the people intended to take that step.*[6]

Hoping to remove the gunpowder in secret and avoid a confrontation, the small British naval detachment entered the capital in the pre-dawn hours of April 21. They had waited several days to do so because the rumors of just such an attempt (which began when Lord Dunmore obtained the key to the powder magazine from the keeper of the magazine) had prompted the Williamsburg volunteer company to post guards on the magazine each night.[7] Such duty in the cold April

---

[5] William B. Clark, "Journal of His Majesty's Schooner Magdalen, April 20, 1775," *Naval Documents of the American Revolution*, Vol. 1, (Washington, D.C., 1964), 204.
[6] K. G. Davies, ed., "Governor Earl of Dunmore to Earl of Dartmouth, May 1, 1775," *Documents of the American Revolution,* Vol. 9, (Irish University Press), 107-108.
[7] John Burk, *The History of Virginia from Its First Settlement to the Present Day*, Vol. 2, (Petersburg, VA: Dickson & Pescud, 1805), 409.

evenings soon grew tiresome and on the evening of April 20, the guards left their post.[8]

This was the opportunity Lord Dunmore had waited for. Informed that the magazine was no longer guarded, Dunmore sent his personal secretary, Captain Edward Foy, with a wagon and the key to the magazine to Burwell's Ferry to alert the British landing party of the *Magdalen* that it was time to proceed.[9] They arrived at the magazine, a two story octagonal brick building constructed in 1715, around 4:00 a.m. To gain access to the magazine they first had to pass through a high brick wall that surrounded the building. The only way to do that was to go through a heavy oak gate that faced the James City Courthouse on Duke of Gloucester Street. As the marines passed through the gate and positioned the wagon to receive the powder, someone in the darkness called out an alarm.[10]

The British landing party had been sighted, perhaps by a frigid sentinel who has sought shelter and warmth nearby, or perhaps from a nearby resident. Whoever it was yelled out for help and the alarm quickly spread. The British marines and sailors moved fast, undeterred by the growing ruckus in the city. With shouts of alarm spreading throughout Williamsburg, they loaded fifteen half barrels of gunpowder onto their wagon and hurried out of town.[11] By the time the citizens of Williamsburg gathered to confront the British party, they were well on their way back to the *Magdalen*. Eager to confront someone for the theft of their gunpowder, the residents of Williamsburg turned

---

[8] Ibid.

[9] Norman Fuss, "Prelude to Rebellion: Dunmore's Raid on the Williamsburg Magazine," *Journal of the American Revolution*, Online.

[10] Ibid.

[11] Kennedy, ed., "Benjamin Waller Testimony," *Journal of the House of Burgesses*: 1773-1776, 232.

their attention to Lord Dunmore. He and his family were only a few hundred yards away in the Governor's Palace.

Lord Dunmore recalled that, "*Drums were then sent through the city,* [and] *the independent company got under arms.*"[12] Anxious city residents gathered at the courthouse in the dim light of dawn and learned what had happened. Benjamin Waller recalled that, "*the People…were much alarmed and assembled some with and others without Arms.*"[13] Attorney General John Randolph who lived close to the magazine and courthouse confirmed that, "*many of the people were under arms at the courthouse,*" and Alexander Purdie's *Virginia Gazette* described the whole city as, "*alarmed and much exasperated….*"[14]

Just around the corner from the courthouse in the Governor's Palace, Lord Dunmore heard the commotion created by the agitated crowd. He reported to the British Ministry after the incident that,

> *All the people assembled and during their consultation continued threats were brought to my house that it was their resolution to seize upon or massacre me and every person found giving me assistance if I refused to deliver the powder immediately into their custody.*[15]

Dunmore's concern for his safety may have been justified; Purdie's gazette reported that, "*numbers got themselves in*

---

[12] Davies, ed., "Governor Earl of Dunmore to Earl of Dartmouth, May 1, 1775," *Documents of the American Revolution,* Vol. 9, 107-108.

[13] Kennedy, ed., "Benjamin Waller Testimony," *Journal of the House of Burgesses*: 1773-1776, 231-32.

[14] Kennedy, ed., "John Randolph Testimony," *Journal of the House of Burgesses*: 1773-1776, 233 and Purdie, *Virginia Gazette Supplement*, April 21, 1775, 3.

[15] Davies, ed., "Dunmore to Dartmouth, May 1, 1775," *Documents of the American Revolution,* Vol. 9, 108.

readiness to repair to the palace."[16] Luckily for Dunmore, Peyton Randolph and other respected leaders of the city were able to calm the irate crowd and prevent them from marching on the Governor's Palace. Instead, a meeting of the Common Hall (the governing body of the city) was held at the courthouse and after much deliberation, a formal address to the governor was drafted. The address began with an account of the removal of the gunpowder and the assertion of the Common Hall that the powder magazine remained the most secure repository for the powder.

> *We, his majesty's dutiful and loyal subjects, the mayor, recorder, aldermen, and common council of the city of Williamsburg, in common-hall assembled, humbly beg leave to represent to your excellency that the inhabitants of this city were this morning exceedingly alarmed by a report that a large quantity of gunpowder was in the preceding night, while they were sleeping in their beds, removed from the public magazine in this city, and conveyed under an escort of marines on board one of his majesty's armed vessels lying at a ferry on James river.*
>
> *We beg leave to represent to your excellency, that as this magazine was erected at the public expence of this colony, and appropriated to the safe keeping of such munition as should be there lodged from time to time, for the protection and security of the country, by arming thereout such of the militia as might be necessary in case of invasion and insurrection, they*

[16] Purdie, "April 21, 1775," *Virginia Gazette Supplement*, 3.

> *humbly conceive it to be the only proper repository to be resorted to in times of imminent danger.*[17]

The Common Hall also noted that reports of, "*designing persons* [who] *have instilled the most diabolical notions in the minds of our slaves,*" had the city on edge and the Common Hall had, "*for some time past judged it necessary to keep strong patrols on foot.*"[18] Therefore, to have, "*the chief and necessary means of their defence removed* [from the magazine], *was very alarming to the inhabitants.*"[19] The Common Hall concluded their address with a plea to Governor Dunmore.

> *Considering ourselves as the guardians of the city, we therefore humbly desire to be informed by your excellency upon what motives and for what particular purpose the powder has been carried off in such a manner; and we earnestly entreat your excellency to order it to be immediately returned to the magazine.*[20]

A delegation of city leaders, accompanied by Speaker Randolph, went to Dunmore's residence to deliver the address and receive the governor's reply.

Realizing the precarious situation he was in, Governor Dunmore admitted to his superior in England, Lord Dartmouth, after the meeting that,

> *With their armed force at a little distance…I thought proper, in the defenceless state in which I* [found]

---

[17] Scribner, ed., "Municipal Common Hall to Governor Dunmore, April 21, 1775," *Revolutionary Virginia: The Road to Independence* Vol. 3, 54-55.
[18] Ibid.
[19] Scribner, ed., "Municipal Common Hall to Governor Dunmore, April 21, 1775," *Revolutionary Virginia: The Road to Independence* Vol. 3, 54-55.
[20] Ibid.

> *myself, to endeavour to soothe them and answered verbally to the effect that I had removed the powder (lest the Negroes might have seized upon it) to a place of security from whence when I saw occasion I would at any time deliver it to the people.*[21]

Dunmore further explained to the delegation that he had the powder removed before dawn, "*to prevent any alarm*," and that, "*he was surprised to hear the people were under arms on this occasion, and that he should not think it prudent to put the powder into their hands in such a situation.*"[22]

Barely able to contain his anger at what he viewed as, "*one of the highest insults that could be offered to the authority of His Majesty's government*," Dunmore ignored the delegation's warning that his reply would be unsatisfactory to the crowd outside.[23] As the delegation left to deliver his reply, Dunmore prepared for the worst, arming himself and his aides and servants.

To the governor's great surprise and relief, Williamsburg's leaders convinced the assembled crowd at the courthouse that Dunmore's response was satisfactory and they dispersed and returned to their homes without incident.[24] The situation remained calm until evening when, according to Benjamin Waller

> *A Report prevailed that the Marines were landed, and intended to Town;* [the residents] *expressed great*

---

[21] Davies, "Dunmore to Dartmouth, May 1, 1775," *Documents of the American Revolution,* Vol. 9, 108.

[22] Scribner, ed., *Revolutionary Virginia: The Road to Independence* Vol. 3, 55.

[23] Davies, ed., "Dunmore to Dartmouth, May 1, 1775," *Documents of the American Revolution,* Vol. 9, 108.

[24] Kennedy, ed., "Testimony of Mayor John Dixon," *Journal of the House of Burgesses*: 1773-1776, 233.

> *uneasiness and went with their Arms to the Magazine to guard it, but soon dispersed except a few who acted as patrole that Night....*[25]

Although the reported landing of British marines proved to be false, the armed Virginians who gathered at the magazine to challenge the marines demonstrated a degree of resistance to British authority that had not appeared in Virginia since Bacon's Rebellion, nearly a century earlier.

Anger at Dunmore Grows

The following day, Lord Dunmore sparked another uproar when he lost his temper in public and unleashed a verbal tirade against the colonists. Mayor John Dixon, like most of Williamsburg, learned of Dunmore's outburst second hand and noted the impact it had on the capital's inhabitants:

> *The Inhabitants appeared to be in perfect tranquility til a Report was spread by his Excellency's throwing out some threats respecting the Slaves, when there seemed to be great uneasiness but nothing more was done but doubling the usual Patrole...*[26]

Dixon's recollection of Dunmore, "throwing out some threats," was a reference to the governor's chance encounter with Dr. William Pasteur outside the governor's palace. Dr. Pasteur reported that he met the highly agitated governor on the street the morning after the powder was seized and that Dunmore, "*seemed greatly exasperated at the Peoples having been under*

---

[25] Kenney, ed., "Testimony of Benjamin Waller," *Journal of the House of Burgesses*: 1773-1776, 231-232.

[26] Kennedy, "Testimony of Mayor John Dixon," *Journal of the House of Burgesses*: 1773-1776, 233.

Arms."[27] Pasteur assured the governor that many of the people realized the rashness of their actions and regretted it, but Dunmore was not placated and unleashed a tirade in response. Pasteur recalled that

> *His Lordship then proceeded to make use of several rash expressions and said that tho' he did not think himself in Danger yet he understood some injury or insult was intended to be offered to the Captains Foy and Collins,* [Dunmore's aide and the captain of the H.M.S. Magellen] *which he should consider as done to himself as those Gentlemen acted intirely by his particular Directions.... His Lordship then swore by the living God that if a Grain of Powder was burnt at Captain Foy or Captain Collins, or if any Injury or insult was offered to himself, or either of them, that he would declare Freedom to the Slaves, and reduce the City of Williamsburg to Ashes. His Lordship then mentioned setting up the Royal Standard, but did not say that he would actually do it, but said he believed, if he did he should have a Majority of white People and all the Slaves on the side of Government, that he had once fought for the Virginians, and that, by GOD, he would let them see that he could fight against them, and declared that in a short Time, he could depopulate the whole Country.*[28]

Reports of Dunmore's volatile outburst and rash threats spread quickly through Williamsburg, surprising no one and

---

[27] Kennedy, ed., "Testimony of Dr. William Pasteur," *Journal of the House of Burgesses*: 1773-1776, 231.
[28] Ibid., 231.

reinforcing a growing belief among many Virginians that Dunmore cared little for their safety or their interests.

This view was further supported by a letter from London (printed in the local gazettes on the day of the powder incident) that claimed that Lord Dunmore had willfully exaggerated the unrest in Virginia in a letter to the British Ministry in late December in order to alarm the Ministry into action. The London correspondent, (who was likely a member of Parliament who supported the colonists) noted that

> *A scene of greater confusion, misrule, and injustice, cannot be conceived, than is described in a letter of Lord Dunmore's dated Dec. 24, as is now prevailing in the province of Virginia.* [According to Dunmore] *Committees are appointed in every county, to enforce what they call the laws of the Congress...* [and] *Armed companies are raised in every county, to enforce the orders of these committees....*[29]

The negative characterization of Virginia that Dunmore's December letter to the Ministry presented was followed a week later by the publication of a large passage of his actual letter. Dunmore's prediction that, "*The lower class of people... will discover that they have been duped by the richer sort...*" and his claim that, "*The arbitrary proceedings of these committees...cannot fail producing quarrels and dissention...*" outraged many colonists.[30] Clearly Governor Dunmore viewed the colonists, and their opposition to Parliament's policies, with contempt and disdain, and the feeling of the colonists towards Dunmore was becoming mutual.

---

[29] Purdie, "April 21, 1775," *Virginia Gazette, Supplement,* 2.
[30] Purdie, "April 28, 1775," *Virginia Gazette, Supplement,* 3.

Had Virginians been aware of the contents of a letter Lord Dunmore wrote to Lord Dartmouth on May 1, 1775, they would have been even angrier. Declaring the unrest in Virginia over the seized gunpowder an insurrection caused by the rebellious spirit of the people, Dunmore reported that "*parties of armed men were continually coming into town from the adjacent counties…offering fresh insults*," and that, "*2,000 armed men*" in Fredericksburg were preparing to march on the capital to force him to return the powder.[31] Dunmore noted that since he could not, "*make any effectual resistance*," against such an overwhelming force, he had sent his wife and children to a British warship in the York River out of fear for their safety. Dunmore was determined, however, to remain in the capital to assert royal authority and he expected city officials to intervene to stop the marchers from Fredericksburg from entering Williamsburg. Dunmore informed Lord Dartmouth that,

> *I have already signified to the magistrates of Williamsburg that I expect them on their allegiance to fall upon means of putting a stop to the march of the people now on their way before they enter the city, that otherwise I shall be forced and it is my fixed purpose to arm all my own Negroes and receive all others that will come to me whom I shall declare free….*[32]

The Governor added that if the magistrates and loyal Virginians did not, "*repair to my assistance*," he would consider

> *The whole country in an actual state of rebellion and myself at liberty to annoy it by every possible means, and that I shall not hesitate at reducing their houses to*

---

[31] Davies, ed., "Dunmore to Dartmouth, May 1, 1775," *Documents of the American Revolution,* Vol. 9, 109.
[32] Ibid.

> *ashes and spreading devastation wherever I can reach.*[33]

Dunmore confidently concluded his letter to Lord Dartmouth by asserting that

> *I am persuaded that if His Majesty should think proper to add to a small body of troops to be sent here a quantity of arms, ammunition and other requisites for the service, I could raise such a force from among Indians, Negroes and other persons as would soon reduce the refractory people of this colony to obedience.*[34]

Luckily for Lord Dunmore, his views and proposals in his letter to Lord Dartmouth remained undisclosed to the public.

Militia on the March

That was not the case concerning the news of the seized powder in Williamsburg, which spread quickly throughout Virginia and reached Fredericksburg on April 24, the same day that the Spotsylvania Independent Militia Company mustered for drill. The officers of the militia company (Hugh Mercer, Alexander Spotswood, and George Weedon) dispatched messengers to neighboring counties and called for a general muster of militia companies in Fredericksburg on Saturday April 29. Their intention was to form a mounted corps of light horse militia and ride to Williamsburg to recover the stolen gunpowder.[35]

---

[33] Ibid.

[34] Davies, ed., "Dunmore to Dartmouth, May 1, 1775," *Documents of the American Revolution,* Vol. 9, 110.

[35] Clark, ed., *Naval Documents of the American Revolution*, Vol. 1, 214-15.

The Spotsylvania company also sent riders to Williamsburg to learn the latest news. Mann Page Jr. and two other riders reached Williamsburg on Wednesday April 27, and were informed that Peyton Randolph and the city leaders of Williamsburg had the situation well under control. In fact, Speaker Randolph, aware of the volatile temper of the governor, was alarmed to learn of the Spotsylvania militia's planned march to Williamsburg and urged the riders to return to Fredericksburg as quickly as possible to halt the march. Randolph explained his decision in a letter to the militia leaders in Fredericksburg.:

> *His Excellency has repeatedly assured several Respectable Gentlemen, that the Powder shall be Return'd to the Magazine…*[and] *thinks that he acted for the best and will not be compell'd to* [do] *what we have abundant Reason to believe he would cheerfully do, were he left to himself.*[36]

Randolph expressed gratitude for the many offers of assistance that were sent to Williamsburg, including the latest from Fredericksburg, but asserted that the situation had stabilized and was under control:

> *It is our opinion and most earnest request that Matters may be quieted for the present; we are firmly persuaded that perfect Tranquility will be speedily Returned; By pursuing this Course we foresee no Hazard or even inconvenience that can ensue; whereas we are apprehensive…that violent measures*

[36] Scribner, ed., *Revolutionary Virginia: The Road to Independence* Vol. 3, 63-64.

> *may produce effects, which God only knows the consequences of.*[37]

Page returned to Fredericksburg at almost the same time that an express rider from the north with news of bloodshed in Massachusetts (Lexington and Concord) passed through town and alarmed everyone. British regulars had reportedly fired without provocation upon the Massachusetts militia.[38] A second account claimed that 4,000 colonial militia had surrounded a brigade of British troops (1,000 strong) in Lexington and had killed 150 regulars at a loss of 50 of their own men.[39] Clearly, something significant had occurred in Massachusetts and the militia assembled in Fredericksburg must have wondered if the events to the north were in anyway related to their own crisis in Virginia.

Undoubtedly anxious about the news from Massachusetts, a council composed of officers from 14 militia companies (representing 600 mounted militia) listened intently as Speaker Randolph's letter was read aloud. A heated debate on whether to proceed to Williamsburg followed. As Peyton Randolph was probably the most respected man in Virginia, his views held tremendous weight with those assembled and after much discussion it was agreed to heed Randolph's plea and cancel the march to the capital. Instead, the council publicly condemned Lord Dunmore for his actions and pledged to re-assemble at a moment's notice to defend their rights or those of any sister colony that was unjustly invaded.[40]

---

[37] Ibid.

[38] Pinkney, "April 28, 1775," *Virginia Gazette, Supplement*, 2.

[39] Ibid.

[40] Scribner, ed., "Spotsylvania Council, April 29, 1775," *Revolutionary Virginia: The Road to Independence*, Vol. 3, 71.

Word of the cancellation of the march from Fredericksburg was welcomed by many in Virginia, but it was soon overshadowed by new reports in the gazettes. Accounts from England informed Virginians that Parliament had extended its strict trade restrictions (that had been imposed on the New England colonies) to all the colonies. This was Parliament's retaliation for the non-importation and non-exportation associations approved by the Continental Congress in the fall of 1774. Equally disturbing were reports that a royal proclamation issued in March declared the inhabitants of Massachusetts and certain individuals in other colonies, (including Peyton Randolph) actual rebels.[41] Ironically, Randolph was doing everything in his power to calm Virginians and prevent an actual rebellion from erupting in Virginia.

Further reports from Massachusetts about the bloodshed at Lexington and Concord also alarmed Virginians in late April.[42] In the coming weeks further details arrived but did little to clarify the situation. For Virginians like Patrick Henry, however, the initial reports of bloodshed in Massachusetts, combined with Dunmore's seizure of the gunpowder in Williamsburg, was proof enough of a ministerial plot to subjugate all of the colonies, and he responded with action.

Henry's March on the Capital

Patrick Henry was surprised and disappointed when he learned that the militia gathered in Fredericksburg had cancelled their march on the capital. A week earlier, Henry had confided to two friends, Richard Morris and George Dabney, that Dunmore's seizure of the powder was a fortunate circumstance that would awaken and animate the public.[43] The

---

[41] Pinkney, "April 28, 1775," *Virginia Gazette*, *Supplement,* 1.
[42] Ibid.
[43] Wirt, 137.

news from Fredericksburg suggested that the animated spirit Henry expected in the people had already waned.

Disappointed but determined, Henry delayed his journey to Philadelphia to attend the Second Continental Congress and instead, rode to Newcastle (a small town twenty miles northeast of Richmond along the Pamunkey River) to meet with the Hanover county committee and Hanover's independent militia company.[44] Charles Dabney attended the meeting and recalled years later that the militia waited most of the day for the committee to decide what to do, "*there being some disagreement among them….*"[45]

In the late afternoon of May 2, Patrick Henry delivered a powerful address to the militia that convinced them to march on to Williamsburg.[46] Reinforced by volunteers from New Kent and King William counties, Henry and the assembled militia (totaling over 150 men) marched to Doncastle's Ordinary, sixteen miles north of Williamsburg.

Fearful that Henry and his men would appear in the capital at any moment, Governor Dunmore hastily prepared for battle. Captain Montague of the recently arrived warship H.M.S. *Fowey* rushed 43 men armed with swords, cutlasses, and bayonets (but no muskets) to the palace and threatened to bombard Yorktown if they were confronted or harassed on their march to Williamsburg.[47] They joined Dunmore's tiny force of armed servants at the palace. The governor also placed cannon

---

[44] Note: Newcastle was a bustling colonial community and a crossing point over the Pamunkey River in Hanover County that has since completely disappeared.

[45] "Charles Dabney to William Wirt, Dec. 21, 1805," *Papers of Patrick Henry* Rockefeller Library CWF, Microfilm.

[46] Wirt, 138.

[47] Pinkney, "May 4, 1775," *Virginia Gazette.*

before the palace and swore to fire on the town should Henry's troops dare enter.[48]

Henry, still at Doncastle's Ordinary, initially dismissed several appeals from Williamsburg's leaders to disband and turn back, but when Carter Braxton arrived in camp and proposed to ride to Williamsburg to convince his father-in-law, Richard Corbin, the receiver-general (tax collector for the King) to issue payment for the powder, Henry agreed to await the outcome of Braxton's efforts. With the help of Thomas Nelson Sr., the respected president of the governor's council, Braxton returned on May 4, with a bill of exchange for 330 pounds to pay for the gunpowder. Henry declared success and pledged to deliver the money to the Virginia delegation in Congress who would use it to purchase gunpowder in Philadelphia for the colony.[49] He then dismissed the troops under his command to their homes and returned to Scotchtown (his home) to prepare for his journey to Philadelphia to attend the Second Continental Congress.

Just two days later, a relieved but angry Governor Dunmore issued a proclamation that essentially declared Patrick Henry and his followers outlaws.

> *Whereas...a certain Patrick Henry...and a Number of deluded Followers, have taken up Arms, chosen their officers, and styling themselves an Independent Company, have marched out of their County, encamped, and put themselves in a Posture of War, and have written and dispatched Letters to* [many] *Parts of the Country, exciting the People to join in these outrageous and rebellious Practices, to the great*

---

[48] Scribner, ed., *Revolutionary Virginia: The Road to Independence* Vol. 3, 9.

[49] Wirt, 142.

> *Terror of all his Majesty's faithful Subjects, and in open Defiance of Law and Government*…[I charge] *all Persons, upon their Allegiance, not to aid, abet, or give Countenance to, the said Patrick Henry, or* [his followers] *but, on the Contrary, to oppose them and their Designs by every Means*….[50]

Dunmore's proclamation had little effect. In fact, it sparked a wave of support for Henry, who was praised by numerous county committees and was safely escorted northward to Maryland by parties of enthusiastic militia.

Although Henry's march on Williamsburg dominated the attention of many Virginians in early May, disturbing details of the bloodshed at Lexington and Concord soon regained their attention. The Virginia gazettes printed numerous accounts in May of the fighting in Massachusetts as well as the militia's "siege" of Boston. The reports varied greatly and described a confused situation.[51]

In the weeks following Patrick Henry's march, Dunmore was strongly criticized by county committees throughout Virginia for his actions, some proclaiming that he had forfeited his right to govern the colony. Distrust of the governor was so high that some suggested that his summons to convene the House of Burgesses on June 1, (specifically to consider a reconciliation proposal from the British Ministry) might really be a ploy to arrest colonial leaders.[52]

Such concerns prompted the Williamsburg Independent Militia company to meet Peyton Randolph (who returned from Philadelphia in late May to resume his seat as Speaker of the

---

[50] Scribner, ed., *Revolutionary Virginia: The Road to Independence* Vol. 3, 100-101.

[51] Purdie, "May 12, 1775," *Virginia Gazette, Supplement,* 1.

[52] John Selby, *The Revolution in Virginia: 1775-1783*, (Colonial Williamsburg Foundation, 1988), 41.

House of Burgesses) outside of town and escort him into the capital with great fanfare. Guards were also posted at the Speaker's home in the center of Williamsburg to ensure his safety.[53]

Collapse of Royal Government

After weeks of tension and crisis in the capital, Lord Dunmore had no desire to provoke another incident by threatening Speaker Randolph or any of the members of the House of Burgesses. Similar consideration was not shown by some of the burgesses who attended the assembly clad in the same course linen hunting shirts (tomahawks at their sides) that were worn by the militia.[54] Despite the defiance conveyed by such attire, the opening session of the House of Burgesses went smoothly, highlighted by Dunmore's address to the assembly in which he endorsed Parliament's reconciliation plan and laid the responsibility for calming the long running dispute on the burgesses. Dunmore defended Parliament's past actions and explained that all that was desired by the King and the, "*supreme legislature of the Empire*" was for the colonies to pay their fair share of the burden of operating the empire.[55] Governor Dunmore noted that under Parliament's plan the colonists were left to decide for themselves a fair amount to contribute to the operation of the empire and if they accepted the plan, it would be, "*Considered by his Majesty not only a Testimony of your Reverence for Parliament, but also as a Mark of your Duty and Attachment to our Sovereign….*"[56] The governor concluded with an appeal to the burgesses.

---

[53] Pinkney, "June 1, 1775," *Virginia Gazette,* 3.
[54] Davies, ed., Dunmore to Dartmouth, June 25, 1775, *Documents of the American Revolution,* Vol. 9, 200-201.
[55]Kennedy, ed., "June 1, 1775," *Journal of the House of Burgesses*: 1773-1776, 174-75.
[56] Ibid.

> *I cannot conclude without exhorting you in the most earnest manner, to enter upon the Subject Matter, now recommended to you, with that Patience, Calmness, and Impartiality, which its great Importance requires, and to reflect upon the Benefits this Country hath received from the Support given to it by the Parent State, which I hope will animate your Zeal, now* [that] *you have it in your Power, to restore that Harmony and mutual confidence which rendered both Countries flourishing, and, in short, to pursue your true Interest, which will convert our present gloomy Apprehensions into Prospects of Peace, Happiness, and lasting Security.*[57]

Although it took the House of Burgesses nearly two weeks to adopt an official reply to Parliament's reconciliation plan, the assembly responded to Dunmore's address within days and asserted that the crisis between England and the colonies was the result of the, "*Departure of his Majesty's Ministers from that wise System of Administration,*" of past years.[58] In other words, the crisis of the last decade was all the fault of the British Ministry and their unconstitutional policies, begun in 1765 and carried to the present. The burgesses also took a swipe at Dunmore for consistently misleading the Ministry about the situation in Virginia:

> *However strangely this Country may have been misrepresented, we do solemnly avow the firmest and most unshaken Attachment to our most gracious*

[57] Ibid.
[58] Kennedy, ed., "June 5, 1775," *Journal of the House of Burgesses*: 1773-1776, 187-88.

> *Sovereign and his Government, as founded on the Laws and Principles of our excellent Constitution.*[59]

The House assured Dunmore that they would fully consider Parliament's reconciliation plan. Many Virginians viewed it, however, for what it was, a scheme to split the colonies, and Speaker Randolph wanted to defer to the Continental Congress for a decision.[60] Unity among the colonies was crucial and Randolph was determined to maintain it, so he delayed action on the proposal. As it turned out, a new crisis at the powder magazine seized everyone's attention and led to an irrevocable break between Dunmore and Virginia's elected representatives.

On the night of June 3, a party of young men broke into the powder magazine to retrieve weapons. A blast from a spring loaded musket showered them with shot. Pellets struck one youth in the arm and shoulder, seriously wounding him and another lost two fingers on his right hand.[61] The city was once again alarmed and many were outraged when they learned that spring guns (set to fire by a trip wire) had been secretly placed in the magazine. Purdie's gazette declared that, "*had any person lost his life, the perpetrator or perpetrators, of this diabolical invention, might have been justly branded with the…title of MURDERERS!*"[62] Pinkney's gazette pointed a finger straight at Dunmore, noting that, "*His lordship has displayed the most profound skill as an engineer…and it is imagined the adventure at the magazine on Saturday night, will be transmitted to the ministry as…proof of the expedience and efficacy of spring guns.*"[63]

---

[59] Ibid.

[60] Selby, *The Revolution in Virginia: 1775-1783,* 42.

[61] Dixon and Hunter, "June 10, 1775," *Virginia Gazette,* 2.

[62] Purdie, "June 9, 1775," *Virginia Gazette Supplement*, 2.

[63] Pinkney, "June 8, 1775," *Virginia Gazette,* 3.

The spring guns proved to be of limited deterrence, however, for two days later a large crowd gathered at the magazine and in the presence of a few burgesses broke in and carted away muskets and other military stores. A committee from the House of Burgesses approached Dunmore and requested that he instruct the Keeper of the Magazine to give them access so that they might examine the state of the magazine, but the governor, angered by what he saw as collusion between the burgesses and those who broke into the magazine, rejected the request, claiming that it had been improperly submitted.

A report spread through the city the next day (Tuesday June 6) that a party of marines and sailors from the H.M.S. *Fowey* were marching to the governor's palace per his orders.[64] Realizing that many of the inhabitants of Williamsburg were, "*determined to attack the said Marines and Sailors if they should come*," members of the governor's council urged Dunmore to order the landing party back to their ship.[65] Dunmore professed surprise that they were coming and agreed that if they were, he would send them back. At the same time, the House of Burgesses ordered Captain James Innes of the Volunteer Company, "*to employ any number of Men, that he shall think sufficient, to guard the public Magazine in this City….*"[66] Alas, the dreaded British marines and sailors never arrived and it is unclear whether they were ever sent. What is clear is that Lord Dunmore had had enough of the disorder.

---

[64] Kennedy, ed., "June 6 1775," *Journal of the House of Burgesses*: 1773-1776, 198.
[65] Ibid.
[66] Ibid.

Dunmore Flees

A tense calm settled upon the capital on Wednesday, June 7, prompted in part by Governor Dunmore's new found cooperative attitude (he granted a committee from the House of Burgesses access to the magazine) and a resolution passed by the burgesses that thanked the governor for his service against the Indians on the frontier in 1774.[67] In the evening, Lord Dunmore walked across town unmolested to visit one of his strongest supporters, John Randolph. There is no record of what they discussed, but it is likely that Dunmore either learned of or informed Randolph that the Virginia gazettes were going to print more damning excerpts of Dunmore's December 24, letter to Lord Dartmouth. The new excerpts, which were included in a letter from a correspondent in London that reached Virginia in early June, painted Lord Dunmore in the worst possible light:

> *Extract from a Letter from London*
>
> *After lord Dunmore had given his uncandid representation of Virginia, as transmitted to you* [earlier], *he proceeded warmly to recommend to lord Dartmouth that some men-of- war* [ships] *should be stationed in Chesapeake Bay, to prevent the Virginians from carrying on any external trade, except with this country, and that all communication might be cut off between them and the northern colonies….* [Dunmore]*…observed that the COUNCIL, as well as the HOUSE OF BURGESSES, and almost EVERY PERSON OF FORTUNE AND CONSIDERATION IN THE COLONY except the ATTORNEY GENERAL*

---

[67] Kennedy, ed., "June 7, 1775," *Journal of the House of Burgesses*: 1773-1776, 199, 201.

> [John Randolph], *were* [as] *deeply engaged as the inferior planters in factious associations and plans of resistance, great outrages and disorders would soon take place among them, from the want of regular distribution of law; and therefore he strongly urged the king's ministers, as a sure method to increase their disorders, and which…could not fail to produce petitions from the RICH, praying for protections of* [Parliament], *that his majesty would, without delay, order HIMSELF, and all the other EXECUTIVE OFFICERS of Virginia, to withdraw from thence….*[68]

The London correspondent concluded with the suggestion that Lord Dunmore was a chief cause of the ongoing political crisis. "*Can you therefore, my dear sir, wonder that* [the Ministry] *perseveres in their ruinous and despotic system of American politics*?"[69]

Given all the unrest that had occurred to date and that was sure to follow after the publication of this letter, Dunmore decided that it was time to withdraw to the safety of the H.M.S. *Fowey*. Early in the morning of June 8, Dunmore and his family, (who had temporarily returned to the palace) accompanied by Captain Foy and his wife and a few of Dunmore's household servants, left the palace and made their way to the British schooner *Magdalen*, anchored a mile and a half away in Queen's Creek. From there they sailed to the York River where Dunmore and his party transferred to the larger H.M.S. *Fowey*, anchored off Yorktown. Dunmore justified his decision to leave the capital in a letter to Lord Dartmouth a few weeks later:

---

[68] Pinkney, "June 8, 1775," *Virginia Gazette,* 3.
[69] Ibid.

> *My house was kept in continual alarm and threatened every night with an assault. Surrounded therefore as I was by armed men in the very place of my residence and in the neighborhood, who were raised in defiance of my authority and pay no obedience to it but assemble and act as their will directs, nor are they to be controlled even by the power which they are intended to support; and situated so far from any place where men-of-war can approach, the nearest being five miles, I could not think it safe to continue any longer in that city but judged it would be best in all respects for carrying on His Majesty's service to remove to the ship of war which is stationed here, where I have for the present fixed my residence and where most probably I shall be obliged to remain until I receive His Majesty's instructions.*[70]

To his credit, Dunmore delivered a similar, albeit more dramatic, explanation for his departure to the House of Burgesses:

> *Being now fully persuaded that my Person, and those of my Family likewise, are in constant danger of falling sacrifices to the blind and unmeasurable fury which has so unaccountably seized upon the minds and understanding of great numbers of People, and apprehending that at length some of them may work themselves up to that pitch of daringness and atrociousness as to fall upon me, in the defenceless state in which they know I am in the City of Williamsburg, and perpetrate Acts that would plunge*

---

[70] Davis, ed., "Dunmore to Dartmouth, June 25, 1775," *Documents of the American Revolution,* Vol. 9, 201-02.

> *this country into the most horrid calamities, and render the breach with the mother Country irreparable, I have thought it prudent…that I remove to a place of safety.*[71]

For their part, the House of Burgesses expressed shock and dismay at Dunmore's actions, displaying a fair degree of amnesia regarding the unrest that had gripped the capital over the preceding month:

> *We…assure your Excellency, that it is with the greatest concern we find…that your Lordship entertains any suspicions of the personal security of yourself or family, as we can by no means suppose any of his Majesty's subjects in this Colony would meditate a crime so horrid and atrocious as you seem to apprehend.*[72]

The House then criticized the governor, assured him that they desired order as much as he did, and pledged to do whatever was necessary to ensure his safety and that of his family:

> *We are fearful the step your Lordship hath taken, in removing from the seat of government, may* [cause] *a continuance of that great uneasiness which hath of late so unhappily prevailed in this Country. We cannot but express our concern that your Lordship did not think proper to communicate the ground of your uneasiness to us, as, from our zeal and attachment to the preservation of order and good government, we*

---

[71]Kennedy, ed., "June 8, 1775," *Journal of the House of Burgesses*: 1773-1776, 206.
[72] Ibid., 207.

> *should have judged it our indispensable duty to have endeavoured to remove every cause of disquietude.... We assure your Lordship that we will cheerfully concur in any measure that may be proposed proper to the security of yourself and your family*...[and] *earnestly entreat your Lordship...to return, with your Lady and family, to the Palace; which we are persuaded will give the greatest satisfaction, and be the most likely means of quieting the minds of the People.*[73]

Dunmore's reply was read to the House of Burgesses two days later. He reiterated that the, "*commotions among the People and their menaces and threats*," and the unsupportive conduct of the burgesses which often countenanced, "*the violent and disorderly proceedings of the People, were the chief cause of his flight*."[74] The governor was also upset with the threats directed at the King's forces on June 6, and the apparent usurpation of his executive authority by the House of Burgesses when they instructed the independent militia company to guard the magazine:[75]

> *When a body of Men assembled in the City of Williamsburg...with the approbation of everybody for the avowed purpose of attacking a party of the Kings forces, which, without the least foundation, it was reported were marching to my protection, and which, if true, ought to have been approved and aided, not opposed and insulted, by all good and loyal Subjects;*

---

[73] Kennedy, ed., "June 8, 1775," *Journal of the House of Burgesses*: 1773-1776, 207.
[74] Kennedy, ed., "June 10, 1775," *Journal of the House of Burgesses*: 1773-1776, 214-15.
[75] Ibid.

> *when especially the House of Burgesses...has ventured upon a step fraught with the most alarming consequences, in ordering and appointing guards, without even consulting me, to mount in the city of Williamsburg, as is pretended, to protect the Magazine* [which] *shews a design to usurp the executive power... I submit it to your own judgement whether I could reasonably expect any good effect from communicating the ground of my uneasiness to you.*[76]

Dunmore accepted the burgesses offer to, "*cheerfully concur to any measure*," that would ensure his security and proposed five measures he wished to see the House implement:

1. Reopen the civil courts.
2. Disarm and dismiss the independent militia companies.
3. Demand the return of the stolen arms and equipment from the public magazine.
4. Stop harassing supporters of the government.
5. Accept Lord North's Olive Branch reconciliation plan.[77]

The House of Burgesses, of course, had no intention of implementing any of Dunmore's proposed measures. Instead, the burgesses adopted an address to Lord Dunmore on June 12, that rejected Parliament's reconciliation plan:

> *With pain and disappointment we must ultimately declare* [the plan] *only changes the form of oppression, without lightening its burden, we cannot,*

---

[76] Ibid.
[77] Ibid., 215.

my Lord, close with the terms of that Resolution for these Reasons.[78]

First, the burgesses declared, "*the British Parliament has no right to intermeddle with the support of civil Government in the Colonies. For us, not for them, has government been instituted.*"[79] Next, the burgesses noted that to obtain Parliament's exemption from unjust taxes, "*we must saddle ourselves with a perpetual tax adequate to the expectations...of Parliament alone.*"[80] In other words, Parliament's proposal would not give the colonists a real choice of whether to contribute an annual payment, such payments were a foregone conclusion.

The burgesses also objected to the fact that the plan did not repeal all the offensive acts passed by Parliament in 1774 or address the enormous military build-up in Massachusetts, which they asserted could only be meant to coerce the colonists into submission.[81] Another objection was the continuation of Britain's trade monopoly over the colonies, something the colonists had previously accepted as their contribution to the British empire. The burgesses claimed that if they were to now make annual contributions to the common defense and civil governance of the colonies, they should be free of the restrictive Navigation Acts and be allowed to trade freely just as their brethren in England were free to do.[82] Lastly, the burgesses reminded Lord Dunmore that they,

---

[78] Kennedy, ed., "June 12, 1775," *Journal of the House of Burgesses*: 1773-1776, 219.
[79] Ibid.
[80] Ibid.
[81] Ibid.
[82] Kennedy, ed., "June 12, 1775," *Journal of the House of Burgesses*: 1773-1776, 220.

> *Consider ourselves as bound in honor as well as interest to share one general fate with our Sister Colonies, and should hold ourselves base deserters of that union...were we to agree on any measures distinct and apart from them.*[83]

In other words, the House of Burgesses placed a high premium on continental unity and deferred to the will of the Continental Congress, which was still wrestling with the plan.

The burgesses' rejection of Parliament's "olive branch" plan marked the end of reconciliation efforts in Virginia. The House of Burgesses met for two more weeks, but Dunmore's refusal to approve or even respond to any of the legislation meant that their efforts to pass laws were futile. They adjourned in frustration on June 24, and most of the burgesses headed home.

As if to cement the rupture between the Virginians and Lord Dunmore, a considerable body of men raided the governor's palace that same evening, breaking in a window and then forcing open the front door despite the objections of Dunmore's remaining staff. The intruders seized nearly 300 stand of arms from the main hallway (muskets, cartridge boxes, bayonets and scabbards) as well as a number of Lord Dunmore's personal weapons.[84] Dunmore's residence was raided again nearly two weeks later on July 6, once again to seize weapons. All of the locks to the doors, cabinets, and private places were smashed and the remainder of Lord Dunmore's personal collection of weapons were taken.[85]

---

[83] Ibid.
[84] Scribner ed., "An Introductory Note," *Revolutionary Virginia: The Road to Independence*, Vol. 3, 223.
[85] Ibid., 224

Williamsburg Becomes and Armed Camp

Prior to these incidents, reports of the possible arrival of 2,000 British troops to Virginia alarmed the inhabitants of Williamsburg.[86] They met at the courthouse on June 23, at the request of Speaker Randolph, to discuss how they should respond to this threat.

> *Last Friday there was a very full meeting of the inhabitants of this city at the courthouse, convened there by desire of our representative, the Hon. Peyton Randolph Esq. to consider of the expedience of stationing a number of men here for the publick safety, as well as to assist the citizens in their nightly watches, to guard against any surprise from our enemies; when it was unanimously agreed (until the General Convention meets, who no doubt will provide against every contingency) to invite down, from a number of counties, to the amount of 250 men, who are expected in a very few days. Meanwhile, until they arrive, the neighboring counties are kind enough to lend us their assistance, the James City volunteers having furnished us with a guard on Wednesday, a party of the New Kent volunteers did duty last night, and this day we expect another detachment from that county, as well as a number of the York volunteers.*[87]

Lord Dunmore observed the increased military activity in Williamsburg and interpreted it as evidence of a deepening rebellion. In a letter to Lord Dartmouth in England, Dunmore described the garrison atmosphere of the city.

---

[86] Dixon and Hunter, "June 24, 1775," *Virginia Gazette*, 2.
[87] Purdie, "June 30, 1775," *Virginia Gazette, Supplement*, 1.

> *A constant guard is kept in Williamsburg relieved every day from the adjacent Counties, and that place is become a Garrison, the pretence of which is the Security of the Person of their Speaker, who because he has been Chairman of the Congress, it is reported, (in order to inflame), that Government is anxious to Seize him.*[88]

By the first week of July, 170 militia volunteers from several counties outside of the area had marched to Williamsburg to join the militia guarding the capital and by mid-July, volunteers from the counties of Goochland, Louisa, Spotsylvania, Albemarle, King George, Stafford, and Williamsburg brought the number of militia on duty in Williamsburg to the full complement of 250.[89]

Alexander Purdie described the volunteers in his gazette as, "*all hearty clever fellows, and ready to take a crack with any ministerial troops that may be sent to molest us.*"[90] The officers assembled in Williamsburg chose Captain Charles Scott of Cumberland County to command them. He was a veteran of the French and Indian War who, according to Purdie's gazette, "*served...in the Virginia regiment with great reputation, and is an excellent woodsman.*"[91]

Never one to shy away from conflict, Lord Dunmore was also eager for a fight, but he lacked sufficient force to act. In late June, he sent his wife and children back to Britain aboard the H.M.S. *Magdalen*, but he remained aboard the H.M.S. *Fowey*, anchored off Yorktown, where he dutifully reported to

---

[88] Clark, ed., "Dunmore to Dartmouth, June 27, 1775," *Naval Documents of the American Revolution*, Vol. 1, 764.
[89] Purdie, "July 7, 1775, 3 and July 14, 1775," *Virginia Gazette, Supplement,* 2.
[90] Purdie, "July 14, 1775," *Virginia Gazette, Supplement,* 2.
[91] Ibid.

Lord Dartmouth in England on the increasingly militant situation in the colony:

> *The People of Virginia manifest open Rebellion by every means in their power, and they declare at the Same time that they are his Majesty's Most dutyfull Subjects…and that as designs have never been formed against my person, but that I may, whenever I please return to my usual Residence without the least danger; notwithstanding that my own Servants are prevented from passing with provisions which is thus cut off from me & denied to me, my people have been Carried off by the guard,; while my house has been a third time rifled, and is now entirely in the possession of these lawless Ruffians. A great number of people, horse and Foot, from various parts of the country have flocked to Williamsburg, armed and accoutered, and wearing uniforms…. They have made a Barrack of the Capitol…and they have taken possession of the Park* [adjoining the Governor's Palace].[92]

The governor himself was nearly carried off in early July in a close encounter with a party of militia at his farmhouse (Porto Bello) on Queen's Creek, just a few miles outside of Williamsburg.[93]

Captain Scott undoubtedly viewed the situation in Williamsburg much differently than Lord Dunmore, but he may have sympathized with the Governor's characterization of the militia in the capital as "*lawless ruffians*." for Scott had a difficult time maintaining proper military discipline among the

---

[92] Clark, ed., "Dunmore to Dartmouth, July 12, 1775," *Naval Documents of the American Revolution,* Vol. 1, 873.
[93] Ibid.

largely untrained and untried militia encamped east of the capitol at Waller's Grove.

Lieutenant George Gilmer of Albemarle County believed a large part of the problem was with Captain Scott himself and expressed this view to his friend, Thomas Jefferson. Gilmer informed Jefferson that he respected Captain Scott, "*who's goodness and merit is great,*" but that Scott possessed a, "*fear to offend,*" that resulted in the largely idle militia troops becoming, "*rather disorderly.*"[94] "*We appear rather invited to feast than fight," complained a frustrated Gilmer; Anderson and Southall's* [taverns] *entertain elegantly – the first in the best manner by far.*"[95]

The surprising departure of Lord Dunmore and the British warships from the York River (they sailed to Norfolk on July 15) made Captain Scott's task even more difficult. With the threat to Williamsburg reduced, drill and guard duty in the capital grew mundane. Men who knew little of military discipline chafed at the repetition of drill and the inactivity of camp life and some fell into mischief. A council of officers finally adopted a set of regulations to instill greater discipline, but it had little effect.

> *Resolutions Adopted by the Officers at Williamsburg, July 18, 1775*
>
> *Resolved, That any private who may refuse when commanded on duty, or...deserts his post, goes to*

---

[94]R.A. Brock, ed., "George Gilmer to Thomas Jefferson, July 1775," in Papers, Military and Political, 1775-1778 of George Gilmer, M.D. of Pen Park, Albemarle Co., VA," *Miscellaneous Papers 1672-1865 Now First Printed from the Manuscripts in the Virginia Historical Society,* (Richmond, VA, 1937), 101.

[95] Ibid.

sleep or absents himself without leave of his officer, shall be punished as follows:

For the first offence, he shall receive a reprimand from his own officer; for the second, that of the Commander-in-Chief before the whole battalion; and for the third, expulsion.

Resolved, That any person who shall fire a gun without leave from the Commanding Officer, shall be taken into custody by the Officer of the Guard and there kept two hours without victuals or drink.[96]

Not surprisingly, such light punishments had little effect on the troops, and the misconduct continued.

Lieutenant Gilmer and his fellow officers also demonstrated poor discipline (and judgment) in late July when they acted on their own initiative to seize funds that were still held by the crown's revenue collector. When the Third Virginia Convention, meeting in Richmond, learned of the militia's unilateral action to seize the funds, it conveyed its strong disapproval and ordered the troops to desist in their actions. The chastised officers humbly responded with an appeal to the Convention to, "*lay down some certain line for our conduct, lest in our excessive zeal we should precipitate our Countrymen into unnecessary Calamities.*"[97]

Dunmore's departure to Norfolk and the convening of the Third Virginia Convention in Richmond created a rather confused situation for the residents of Williamsburg in July and August as many miles separated Williamsburg from those two

---

[96] Brock, ed., "Resolutions Adopted by the Officers at Williamsburg, July 18, 1775," *Gilmer Papers*, 92-93.

[97] Brock, ed., "To the President and Gentlemen of the Convention" *Gilmer Papers*, 109.

locations. The attention of Virginians naturally shifted away from the capital, to Norfolk and Richmond, where Dunmore and the Third Convention both prepared for war.

Third Virginia Convention

The Third Virginia Convention had been in session in Richmond for two weeks when the militia officers in Williamsburg appealed to the delegates for more guidance and regulation. The Convention had made progress on a detailed plan to restructure Virginia's military forces, but it took most of August to finish the job. The plan they adopted replaced the volunteer militia companies with a combination of regular (full time) soldiers and militia soldiers. Two regiments of regular troops, similar to the Virginia regiments raised in the French and Indian War, would be recruited to serve for one year. Patrick Henry was selected to command the first regiment, which consisted of eight 68 man companies and totaled 544 men.[98] Colonel William Woodford, of Caroline County, commanded the second regiment, which comprised 476 men in seven companies.[99] To raise this force, the Convention divided Virginia into sixteen districts and ordered each district (comprised of several counties) to recruit and send their company of regulars to Williamsburg as soon as possible.[100] The company of regulars from the eastern shore of Virginia remained there as a detached unit to help protect this isolated and vulnerable region of the colony.

The regular troops were not the only soldiers ordered to Williamsburg; hundreds of minutemen were ordered to march to the capital as well. They comprised a second tier of

---

[98] William W. Hening, ed., *The Statutes at Large Being a Collection of all the Laws of Virginia,* Vol. 9, (Richmond: J. & G. Cochran, 1821), 9.
[99] Ibid., 10.
[100] Ibid., 10, 16.

Virginia's new military establishment. The Convention authorized sixteen battalions of minutemen. These men were drawn from the ranks of the militia and were "*more strictly trained to proper discipline*" than the ordinary militia.[101] Each of the sixteen districts were ordered to raise a 500 man battalion of minutemen "*from the age of sixteen to fifty, to be divided into ten companies of fifty men each."*[102] Like the regular troops, the minutemen were provided with proper arms as well as a hunting shirt and leggings.[103]

The last tier of Virginia's new military establishment was the traditional county militia. The Convention decreed that

> *All male persons, hired servants, and apprentices, above the age of sixteen, and under fifty years...shall be enlisted into the militia...and formed into companies....*[104]

The militia companies were ordered to hold private musters every two weeks, except in the winter.

The restructuring of Virginia's military forces meant that the volunteer and independent companies that had formed within the last year had reached the end of their tenure. They were created to fill a gap that existed with the expiration of the Militia Law of 1771 and now both the volunteer companies, and the old militia law, were made obsolete by the Third Virginia Convention's new military establishment. The Convention ordered that the volunteer companies should be disbanded as soon as the new minute battalions were raised.[105] With

---

[101] Ibid., 16.
[102] Ibid., 16-17.
[103] Ibid., 20.
[104] Hening, ed., *The Statutes at Large Being a Collection of all the Laws of Virginia,* Vol. 9, 27-28.
[105] Purdie, "August 25, 1775," *Virginia Gazette,* 4.

enthusiasm to serve running high in Virginia, most of the regular and minute companies were completed quickly.

It appears that several volunteer companies were still in Williamsburg in late August, however, for they turned out at the college on August 25, to welcome and escort Peyton Randolph home from the convention in Richmond.[106] Speaker Randolph hoped to rest for a few days and restore his health before embarking on yet another trip to Philadelphia to attend the Continental Congress in early September.

A few days after Randolph's departure for Philadelphia, a strong hurricane smashed into southeastern Virginia, damaging the entire region. Despite the destruction and loss caused by the storm, it did not divert the attention of Virginians for very long from the conflict with Lord Dunmore. In fact, just days after the storm, an incident occurred with the few remaining volunteer troops in Williamsburg concerning a less then patriotic resident of Williamsburg.

Joshua Hardcastle had apparently uttered, "*expressions highly degrading the good people who compose the several companies*," encamped in Waller's Grove and had, "*frequently spoke of the cause of America in a most disgraceful and menacing manner*."[107] Upon word of such talk, a party of militia volunteers seized Hardcastle and conducted him to their encampment in the Grove where a trial was held. "*After a candid, mature, and deliberate examination of the witness*," Hardcastle was found guilty. Tar and feathers were threatened, but in the end, Hardcastle was forced only to ask his pardon of all the officers and soldiers assembled and promise to never commit such offenses again.[108]

---

[106] Purdie, "August 25, 1775," *Virginia Gazette*, 6.
[107] Pinkney, "September 7, 1775," *Virginia Gazette*, 3.
[108] Ibid.

About a week later, Captain Innes led about 100 volunteers to Hampton upon reports that the H.M.S. *Otter* intended to attack the town. This was likely the last service the volunteer militia troops of 1775 performed, for not long after they departed for Hampton, Colonel Patrick Henry, the commander of the First Virginia Regiment and commander in chief of Virginia's regular forces, arrived in Williamsburg to take command. Colonel Henry's arrival in Williamsburg marked the end of the volunteer companies, many of whose members had already joined either the regular companies or the minute companies being raised in their own communities. From here on out, Williamsburg and the rest of Virginia would be defended by a combination of full-time regular troops and militia, both much better organized than the volunteer companies ever were.

Williamsburg's inhabitants also contributed to their defense, forming two militia companies per the new arrangement of the Third Virginia Convention. The Williamsburg committee formed in late 1774 to enforce the resolutions of the First Continental Congress elected John Dixon, newspaper publisher, city alderman and current mayor of the city as colonel of this small force of two companies. Joseph Hornsby, a prosperous merchant in the city was chosen to serve as major. The committee elected one of its own, James Southall, owner of the Raleigh Tavern, and John Hatley Norton, son of wealthy merchant John Norton, to serve as company captains for each company. Benjamin Carter Waller and William Russell were selected as lieutenants and Joseph Kidd and George Reid were chosen to serve as ensigns.[109] A company of minutemen, raised from troops in Williamsburg

---

[109] Ibid.

and the surrounding counties and commanded by Captain Robert Anderson of Williamsburg, was also formed.[110]

These men represented Williamsburg's new military leadership, but they were not alone. Hundreds of enthusiastic regular troops and minutemen soon arrived to help defend Williamsburg.

---

110 Purdie, "October 6, 1775," *Virginia Gazette*, 3.

Three

War Comes to Virginia: Fall 1775

The task of organizing and regulating the steady stream of troops that arrived in Williamsburg in late September and most of October initially fell to Colonel Thomas Bullit of Prince William County, a French and Indian War veteran and adjutant general of Virginia's regular forces. Colonel Bullit, who joined Colonel Henry in Williamsburg in late September, laid out an encampment behind the college and acted to establish order and discipline among the new troops. Over the ensuing weeks, instruction on rations, arms, ammunition, latrines, guard duty, troop formations, drill, and so on were issued and often repeated by both Colonel Bullit and Colonel Henry in an effort to properly organize the new troops.[1] Most of the military activity was confined to the grounds of the college, where visitors observed an encampment of cloth and wooden tents behind the Wren building and squads of troops drilling several hours a day, some with, some without weapons.[2] Efforts were made to keep the soldiers out of town (and out of trouble) through frequent roll call, drill, and sentries posted about camp.[3] Courts martial to punish offenders were also held when needed.

One issue that concerned Colonel Henry and especially the residents of Williamsburg was the proper conduct of the hundreds of troops in the capital. In early October, Henry

---

[1] Brent Tarter, ed., "General Orders, September 27 – October 8, 1775," "The Orderly Book of the Second Virginia Regiment: September 27, 1775 – April 15, 1776" *The Virginia Magazine of History and Biography*, Vol. 85, No. 2, (April, 1997), 159-163.
[2] Ibid.,
[3] Ibid., "September 28, 1775," 161.

reminded his officers and men that they must, "*preserve Decency and Good order in the Camp, and that Some irregularity now practiced be Reformed with as much haste as young Recruits will admit of.*"[4] While not necessarily a draconian command to reform misbehavior, it demonstrated the anxiety that Henry and his fellow officers felt about the behavior of their young soldiers, many who had never been more than a few miles from their homes.

The steady arrival of additional troops filled the college camp and forced Colonel Henry to quarter soldiers within Williamsburg. It remains unclear where these troops were housed, but Henry's reminder to their officers to make sure that the men quartered in the city were, "*ready on the Parade at the Usual Time of Relieving Guards,*" suggests that he was concerned about their detachment from the camp. [5]

Protecting Williamsburg was an important objective for Colonel Henry. By mid-October, guard posts at Burwell's Ferry on the James River and on Queen's Creek where it joined the York River were established.[6] If Lord Dunmore dared to strike at Williamsburg, these posts would see him sailing up the James or York Rivers and provide some warning.

Whether the troops in Williamsburg were capable of much resistance to an attack, however, was uncertain. Shortages of weapons, shot pouches, powder horns, and most importantly rounds for the men limited their capabilities. Colonel Henry expressed hope in mid-October that each solider could be provided with at least ten cartridges, but it was an enormous struggle to do so, especially with additional troops arriving daily.[7]

---

[4] Ibid., "October, 8, 1775," 164.
[5] Ibid., "October, 20, 1775," 169.
[6] Ibid., "October 12, 1775," 167.
[7] Ibid., "October 13, 1775," 167.

The inhabitants of Williamsburg were undoubtedly overwhelmed by the presence of so many armed men on the outskirts of town and within the city and more than a few likely held mixed feelings about the situation. A young soldier in the Culpeper Minute Battalion captured the view of many in the capital when he noted the local population's reaction to the arrival of his unit on October 20.

> *The people, hearing that we were from the backwoods, and seeing our savage-looking equipment seemed as much afraid of us as if we had been Indians.*[8]

There were economic benefits, however, to having so many troops about the city. The soldiers needed all manner of small clothes, hats, shoes and most particularly hunting shirts, or at least the material to make hunting shirts. The also needed camp gear like kettles and pots, shovels, blankets and tents, not to mention all of the military equipment of soldiers including, firearms, flints, pouches, canteens, etc. Williamsburg's tradesmen and merchants scrambled to fulfill the needs of the troops as best they could.[9]

Providing for the troops ultimately fell to the newly formed Virginia Committee of Safety. Established by the Third Virginia Convention to serve as a governing body for the colony between sessions of the conventions or House of Burgesses (were that body ever to meet again). The Virginia Committee of Safety initially met in Richmond at the end of

---

[8] Reverend Philip Slaughter, *A History of St. Mark's Parish: Culpeper County Virginia*, (1877), 107.

[9] Pinkney, "October 12, 1775," *Virginia Gazette*, 2.

Note: For a thorough accounting of many of the transactions that occurred to supply the troops in Williamsburg, see Gregory Sandor's *Journal of the Public Store at Williamsburg, 1775-1776,* (self-published).

August and moved to Hanovertown in mid-September. In late September, the committee moved permantly to Williamsburg.

Edmund Pendleton of Caroline County, led the committee. He was joined by George Mason, John Page, Richard Bland, Thomas Ludwell Lee, Paul Carrington, Dudley Digges, William Cabell, Carter Braxton, James Mercer, and John Tabb. These eleven men essentially served as Virginia's governing body until the Fourth Virginia Convention met in early December and as such, they authorized payment for the thousands of soldiers being raised in the colony as well as their clothing and equipment. As the governing body of the colony, the committee also exercised authority over Virginia's military forces and issued instructions to Colonel Henry on a regular basis.

While Williamsburg adjusted to the influx of troops about the city, Lord Dunmore remained anchored off Norfolk in the Elizabeth River, protected by several British warships and a small contingent of British soldiers from the Fourteenth Regiment who arrived in August from St. Augustine, Florida. The residents of Williamsburg learned of the arrival of these British troops through their gazettes. Alexander Purdie reported on August 4, that,

> *Lord Dunmore reviewed his 60 body-guardsmen, lately arrived from St. Augustine...at Gosport and we hear, that he daily expects an additional reinforcement, of 40 more soldiers, from the same place.*[10]

Purdie speculated that,

---

[10] Purdie, "August 4, 1775," *Virginia Gazette,* 3.

> *His Lordship it is said, as soon as they arrive, and when joined by the marines from the Mercury and Otter men of war, and a number of other select friends in different places, intends coming round to York town; from whence, if not prevented, it is likely he will pay us a visit in this city, although he cannot expect the same cordial reception as on former occasions, but will probably be received with such illuminations &ct. as may make him forget his way to the palace.*[11]

Purdie confidently added that,

> *The good people of Virginia now consider Lord Dunmore as their mortal enemy, and will no longer brook the many insults they have received from him, which are daily repeated; and the "damn'd shirtmen," as they are emphatically called by some of his minions...will make* [them regret] *before long, their ill-timed, base, and ungenerous conduct.*[12]

Purdie's speculation of Lord Dunmore's intentions was not far off. The governor did indeed desire to strike back at Williamsburg, but he realized he was not yet strong enough to do so. Frustrated by the lack of support he had yet received from his superiors in London, Dunmore wrote to Lord Dartmouth declaring that,

> [Were] *I speedily supplied with a few hundred more* [troops] *with Arms, Ammunition and the other requisites of War, and with full powers to act... I could*

---

[11] Ibid.
[12] Ibid.

in a few months reduce this Colony to perfect Submission.[13]

Alas, no such support was forthcoming, at least from the British army or navy. Dunmore was forced to make do with the few British troops, marines and sailors already on scene in Norfolk.

Dunmore Asserts His Authority

While his small numbers constrained Dunmore's ability to strike at the rebels in Williamsburg, they did not prevent the governor from boldly interjecting his will upon Virginia's largest city, Norfolk, and the surrounding countryside. In late September, Captain Mathew Squire of the H.M.S. *Otter* sent a small landing party into Norfolk with Dunmore's approval to seize John Holt, the printer of Norfolk's only newspaper. Holt had printed several critical accounts of Captain Squire's conduct in the days prior to the raid, so the annoyed captain sent a handful of British marines and sailors ashore to halt Holt's publication. The lack of resistance offered to the British landing party by the inhabitants of Norfolk frustrated Virginia's leaders in Williamsburg. Accounts of the affair in the Williamsburg newspapers spread the shame and criticism of the people of Norfolk throughout the colony.

Yesterday came ashore about 15 of the King's soldiers, and marched up to the printing-office, out of which they took all the types and part of the press and carried them on board the new ship Eilbeck, in presence, I suppose, of between two and three hundred

---

[13] Clark, ed., "Lord Dunmore to Lord Dartmouth, Aug. 2, 1775," *Naval Documents of the American Revolution*, Vol. 1, 1045.

> *spectators, without meeting with the least molestation; and upon the drums beating up and down the town, there were only about 35 men to arms….*[14]

Although the raid failed to capture Mr. Holt, the lack of opposition to Captain Squire's small landing party delighted Lord Dunmore and his supporters. Norfolk's committee tried to salvage the town's tarnished reputation by complaining to Lord Dunmore about the, "illegal and riotous," actions of his landing party but this charge provoked only derision from the governor.[15] Dunmore taunted the committee further with a stinging observation that its claim of self restraint in opposing the landing party was not due to choice, but rather, necessity.[16]

Dunmore's Raids

Emboldened by the timid response of the residents of Norfolk, Lord Dunmore launched a series of raids in mid-October to seize arms and ammunition in the surrounding countryside around Norfolk. Captain Samuel Leslie, the ranking officer of the Fourteenth Regiment in Virginia, led the first raid on October 12, and recalled,

> *I landed the 12th of* [October] *at 11 o'Clock at night about three miles from hence with Lieut. Lawrie, two Serjeants, & forty rank and file of the 14th Regiment, and after marching three miles into the country in search of Artillery we found in a wood nineteen pieces of cannon, some of them twelve, others nine, six &*

---

[14] Clark, ed., "Extract of a Letter from Norfolk, October1, 1775," *Naval Documents of the American Revolution*, Vol. 2, 267.

[15] Clark, ed., "Common Hall of the Borough of Norfolk to Lord Dunmore, 30 September 30, 1775," and "Lord Dunmore to the Town Hall of the Borough of Norfolk, 30 September 30, 1775," *Naval Documents of the American Revolution*, Vol. 2, 258-60.

[16] Ibid., 259-60.

> *three pounders; seventeen of which we destroyed, & brought off two, and then returning to our boats we reimbarked without the least opposition. Lord Dunmore accompanied us upon this expedition.*[17]

Lord Dunmore described the next raid that occurred three days later:

> *On the 15th Instant, I landed with between 70 and 80 Men (which was all we could Spare to take with us) some little distance from* [Norfolk] *in the Night, and Marched about a Mile and a half up the Country, where we destroyed 17 pieces of Ordinance and brought off two more, that the Rebels had carried from…Norfolk, and concealed there.*[18]

More raids followed, prompting Dunmore to brag to Lord Dartmouth on October 22, that

> *On the 20th we landed again and brought off Six more Guns, and Yesterday we landed again and brought off Ten Guns and Two Cohorns, and between fifty and Sixty small Arms and a great quantity of Ball of all Sorts and Sizes, which I believe is all the Military Stores in this Neighborhood that could be of any Service to the Rebels….*[19]

Dunmore also offered his assessment of the impact of the raids on both the rebels and the "friends of government".

---

[17] Clark, ed., "Captain Leslie to General Howe, November 1, 1775," *Naval Documents of the American Revolution*, Vol. 2, 844-45.
[18] Clark, ed., "Lord Dunmore to Lord Dartmouth, October 22, 1775," *Naval Documents of the American Revolution,* Vol. 2, 574-75.
[19] Ibid.

> *I can assure your Lordship that landing in this manner has discouraged exceedingly the Rebels, and has raised the Spirits of the friends of Government so much that they are offering their Services from all quarters.*[20]

Governor Dunmore erred in his assessment of the opposition. Across the water in Hampton a party of Virginians were more than ready to resist Lord Dunmore and the British navy and in doing so, inaugurate bloodshed and war in Virginia.

Battle of Hampton

While Lord Dunmore had employed the Fourteenth Regiment to seize arms and ammunition in Princess Anne County and Norfolk County in October against virtually no opposition, Captain Squire had threatened utter destruction to the inhabitants of Hampton (across the water of Hampton Roads) for an incident that occurred when the hurricane of early September struck. The fierce winds and strong tidal surge of the hurricane had pummeled Dunmore's small fleet in the Elizabeth River and Hampton Roads, grounding several vessels. One of Captain Squire's tenders, a small sloop with the captain aboard, was caught in the storm near Hampton and blown ashore near Back Creek. Most of the crew, including two runaway slaves, were taken into custody by the local militia and the ship's stores were seized before the vessel was burned, but Captain Squire managed to elude the militia and escape into the woods.[21]

---

[20] Ibid.

[21] Pinkney, "September 7, 1775," *Virginia Gazette.*

Upon his return to the *Otter*, Captain Squire sent a message to the Hampton town committee demanding the return of the captured tender and stores.[22] The Hampton Committee forwarded Captain Squire's letter to Williamsburg and included a plea for assistance. This was the impetus for Captain Innes to march from Williamsburg to Hampton with his volunteers in mid-September.[23]

The arrival of troops from Williamsburg bolstered the spirits of Hampton's inhabitants and prompted the town committee to belligerently dismiss Captain Squire's threats and reject his demands. Squire responded by posting armed vessels at the mouth of Hampton's harbor to effectively blockade it.

A stalemate ensued for several weeks until late October when Captain Squire decided to attack and burn Hampton. Defending the town was a company of Second Virginia regulars under the command of Captain George Nicholas, the son of Virginia's treasurer, Robert Carter Nicholas. A company of minute-men and a number of militia from Hampton also defended the town. Early in the morning of October 26, Captain Squire moved against Hampton. An account of the assault appeared in Dixon and Hunter's *Virginia Gazette*.

> [On the morning of Oct. 26th] *there appeared off the mouth of Hampton river a large armed schooner, a sloop, and three tenders, with soldiers on board, and a message was received at Hampton, from Captain Squires, on board the schooner, that he would that day land and burn the town; on which a company of regulars and a company of minute-men, who had been*

---

[22] Clark, ed., "Captain Squire to the Hampton Town Committee, September 10, 1775," *Naval Documents of the American Revolution*, Vol. 2, 74.

[23] Robert L. Scribner and Brent Tarter, eds., *Revolutionary Virginia: The Road to Independence,* Vol. 4, (University Press of Virginia, 1978), 96.

placed there in consequence of former threats...against that place made the best disposition to prevent their landing, aided by a body of militia, who were suddenly called together on the occasion.[24]

According to Lord Dunmore's account of the day's affair, gunfire erupted from the rebels onshore when Captain Squire's tenders approached Hampton harbor:

Some of the King's tenders went pretty close into Hampton Road. So soon as the rebels perceived them, they marched out against them and the moment they got within shot of our people, Mr. George Nicholas...who commanded a party of rebels at that time at Hampton, fired at one of the tenders, whose example was followed by his whole party. The tenders returned the fire but without the least effect.[25]

Dunmore laid the blame for the first shot at Hampton (and thus the inauguration of warfare in Virginia) on Captain Nicholas of the Second Virginia Regiment, but an eyewitness saw the engagement differently. He reported that as the tenders approached Hampton

Two vollies of musquetry were discharged from the tenders, and answered by captain Lyne from his post by a rifle, which was answered by a four pounder from one of the tenders; then began a pretty warm fire from all the tenders. Captain Nicholas, observing this, soon joined about 25 of his men. The fire of our musquetry

---

[24] Dixon and Hunter, "October 28, 1775," *Virginia Gazette,* 3.
[25] Davis, ed., "Lord Dunmore to Lord Dartmouth, December 6, 1775 through February, 1776," *Documents of the American Revolution,* Vol. 3, 58.

> *caused the tender nighest to us to sheer off some distance.*[26]

Captain Lyne of the minute company was identified in a second account as the one, "*who fired the first gun in the attack at the mouth of the river,* [and] *killed a man by that very fire.*"[27]

Whether this meant he fired the very first shot of the engagement is unclear. What is clear is that the two sides fired upon each other for over an hour with the tenders getting the worst of it. Unable to maneuver past the sunken vessels obstructing the harbor, the tenders were raked with rifle and musket fire from shore. Their crews responded with cannon, swivel, and musket fire, but it apparently had little effect on the Virginians, who were well sheltered on shore. One rebel combatant recalled that,

> *The fire* [from the tenders] *consisted of 4 pounders, grape shot etc. for about an hour. Not a man of our's was hurt. Whether our men did any damage is uncertain. They could not get nigher than 300 yards. Some say they saw men fall in one of the tenders.*[28]

The confident rebels attempted to draw the enemy to shore, but Captain Squire would not take the bait.[29] Pinkney's *Virginia Gazette* boasted of the bravery the Virginians displayed against Captain Squire's squadron.

> *No troops could shew more intrepidity than the raw, new raised men, under the command of captain Nicholas, of the second regiment, and captain Lyne, of*

---

[26] Pinkney, "November 2, 1775," 2.
[27] Ibid.
[28] Ibid.
[29] Ibid.

> *the minute men, together with some of the country militia. These brave young officers, at the head of their men, without the least cover or breast-work, on the open shore, stood a discharge of 4 pounders, and other cannon, from a large schooner commanded by captain Squire himself, and from a sloop and two tenders, which played on them with all their guns, swivels, and muskets. They stood cooly till the vessels were near enough for them to do execution, when they began a brisk and well directed fire, which forced the little squadron to retire.*[30]

Although nightfall ended the fighting, both sides remained active. Under cover of darkness and a driving rain the British returned to the sunken obstructions and worked to create a passage through the channel while the rebels strengthened their breastworks on the town wharf and anxiously waited for reinforcements from Williamsburg.

Colonel William Woodford marched all night, not with his own troops from the Second Virginia Regiment, but with a company of riflemen from the Culpeper Minutemen and took command of the rebel forces when he reached Hampton in the morning. In a letter to his friend Thomas Jefferson, John Page, a member of the Committee of Safety, provided a detailed account of events on the second day that were likely provided to him by Colonel Woodford or another rebel officer.

> *Col. Woodford accompanied Captain Buford's rifle company through a heavy rain to Hampton and arrived about 7 a.m. When the Col. Entered the Town, having left the Rifle Men in the Church to dry*

---

[30] Pinkney, "October 26, 1775," *Virginia Gazette,* 3.

themselves, he rode down to the River, took A view of the Town, and then seeing the Six Tenders at Anchor in the River went to Col. Cary's to dry himself and eat his Breakfast. But before he could do either the Tenders had cut their Way through the Vessel's Boltsprit which was sunk to impede their Passage and having a very fresh and fair Gale had anchored in the Creek and abreast of the Town.

The People were so astonished at their unexpected and sudden Arrival that they stood staring at them and omitted to give the Col. the least Notice of their approach. The first Intelligence he had of this Affair was from the Discharge of a 4 Pounder. He mounted his Horse and riding down to the Warf found that the People of the Town had abandoned their Houses and riding down to the Militia had left the Breast Work which had been thrown up across the Wharf and street.

He returned to order down Captn. Nicholas's Company and Buford's and meeting Nicholas's, which had been encamped near Col. Cary's he lead them pulling down the Garden Pails [fence] *through Jones's Garden under Cover of his House, and lodged them in the House directing them to fire from the Window which they did with great Spirit. He then returned and lead Buford's Company in the same manner under Cover of Houses on the other Side of the Street placing some in a House and others at a Breast work on the Shore.*

Here he found the Militia had crowded in, and incommoded the Rifle men. He therefore ordered them off and stationed them with Captn. Lynes on the back of the Town to prevent a surprise, by an Attack of

> *Regulars who it was said had landed at Back water. Captn. Barron with the Town Militia and Part of Nicholas's Company were stationed at the Breast Work on the Wharf and across the Street. The Fire was now general and constant on both Sides. Cannon Balls Grape Shot and Musket Balls whistled over the Heads of our Men, Whilst our Muskets and Rifles poured Showers of Balls into their Vessels and they were so well directed that the Men on Board the Schooner in which Captain Squires himself commanded were unable to stand to their 4 Pounders which were not sheltered by a Netting and gave but one Round of them but kept up an incessant firing of smaller Guns and swivels, as did 2 Sloops and 3 Boats for more than an Hour and ¼ when they slipt their Cables and towed out except the Hawk Tender a Pilot Boat they had taken some Time before from a Man of Hampton, which was* [captured].[31]

Lord Dunmore confirmed much of Page's account in a report to Lord Dartmouth.[32]

News of the success of Virginia's forces at Hampton was a welcome relief to the colony's leaders in Williamsburg. Just prior to the engagement, the Committee of Safety had ordered Colonel Henry to send Woodford and the Second Virginia Regiment, reinforced with several companies of Culpeper Minutemen, across the James River to Norfolk to challenge Lord Dunmore's activities there. The fighting at Hampton interfered with preparations for Woodford's march to Norfolk,

---

[31] Clark, ed., "John Page to Thomas Jefferson, November 11, 1775," *Naval Documents of the American Revolution,* Vol. 2, 991-92.

[32] Davis, ed., "Lord Dunmore to Lord Dartmouth, December 6, 1775 through February, 1776," *Documents of the American Revolution*, Vol. 3, 58.

but a much greater obstacle was the shortage of supplies for his troops.

Upon his return to Williamsburg in late October, Colonel Woodford found his detachment of Second Virginians and Culpeper Minutemen (some 650 strong) unprepared for a march to Norfolk.[33] A shortage of tents, arms, and other supplies was the principle reason, but the sudden arrival of a portion of Lord Dunmore's flotilla off of Burwell's Landing and Jamestown Island (which threatened Williamsburg and obstructed passage over the James River) contributed to the delay. Skirmishes between Dunmore's ships and troops from Colonel Henry's First Virginia Regiment posted onshore occurred daily but failed to drive Dunmore's ships away. Woodford and his detachment were forced to cross the river further north, where it narrowed and where the British tenders were not present.[34]

The Committee of Safety's decision to send Colonel Woodford and the Second Virginia Regiment to Norfolk instead of Colonel Henry and the First Virginia apparently did not sit well with Henry and his officers. They viewed the committee's decision as a slight to both Colonel Henry and themselves. Prior to Woodford's departure for Norfolk, the committee learned of a meeting of Henry's officers (without his presence) to apparently discuss the matter and vent their complaints. The Committee of Safety found this gathering of officers disturbing and expressed their displeasure to Colonel Henry.[35] Fortunately, nothing more came of the matter, but it

---

[33] Julian P. Boyd, ed., "Edmund Pendleton to Thomas Jefferson, November 16, 1775," *The Papers of Thomas Jefferson,* Vol. 1, (Princeton, NJ: Princeton University Press, 1950), 260-61.

[34] Clark, ed., "John Page to Thomas Jefferson, November 11, 1775," *Naval Documents of the American Revolution*, Vol. 2, 991-92.

[35] Scribner and Tarter, eds., "Vice-President John Page to Patrick Henry, November 4, 1775," *Revolutionary Virginia: The Road to Independence,* Vol. 4, 321.

did highlight the tension between Colonel Henry and his supporters and the Committee of Safety.

While Colonel Woodford's detachment marched to Norfolk, the Committee of Safety turned its attention towards accommodating the troops that remained in the capital for the winter. The committee instructed the officers of the First Virginia Regiment to,

> *Have the Capitol* [building] *& such other Houses as to them shall seem necessary & convenient, prepared & put in proper Order for the Reception of the Troops & Minutemen in Winter Quarters, as expeditiously as may be, & remove into such Quarters as soon as the Commanding Officer shall think proper.*[36]

The elegant capitol building where the House of Burgess and the General Court of Virginia met, was to be transformed into winter quarters for Colonel Henry's troops.

As things turned out, there were few troops within Williamsburg over the winter, most were sent across the James River to guard against Lord Dunmore while others were sent to Hampton to stand guard there. With no fireplaces in the capitol (to prevent fires) it is doubtful the capitol was ever used to house troops. The Committee of Safety's instructions to Lieutenant Colonel William Christian (who briefly commanded the troops in Williamsburg in early March 1776) to provide a return of, "*a State of the Houses & rooms occupied as Barracks, the size of each room, its number of Soldiers, and the Quantity of Fuel delivered…*," suggests the troops spent the winter in

---

[36] Scribner and Tarter, eds., "Virginia Committee of Safety, November 8, 1775," *Revolutionary Virginia: The Road to Independence,* Vol. 4, 344.

several buildings in the city.[37] An order to call the roll each day, "*before the door of their Barracks*," also suggests that the troops remained in such accommodations at least through March.[38]

While the Virginia Committee of Safety oversaw such military arrangements and preparations, the freeholders of Williamsburg met on November 9, to renew the local committee formed a year earlier that was charged with implementing the decisions of the First Continental Congress in October 1774. Twenty-one men were selected to serve on the committee for the following year (1776); their names were listed according to the number of votes they received.

James Southall	Robert Carter Nicholas	John Tazewell
James Geddy	Robert Nicholson	William Pasteur
Alexander Craig	Humphrey Harwood	George Wythe
Benjamin Powell	Thomas Everard	Gabriel Maupin
John Galt	Edward Charlton	Joseph Prentis
Joseph Hornsby	James Hubard	William Goodson
Robert Anderson	John Blair	John Ferguson[39]

In early December the Fourth Virginia Convention arrived in Williamsburg to once again serve as the de facto governing body in Virginia. The convention met daily at the college.[40]

---

[37] Scribner and Tarter, eds., "Virginia Committee of Safety, March 5, 1776," *Revolutionary Virginia: The Road to Independence*, Vol. 6, (Charlottesville: University Press of Virginia, 1981), 170-172.

[38] Charles Campbell, ed., "General Orders, March 28, 1776," *The Orderly Book of the Portion of the American Army Stationed at or Near Williamsburg...March 18 to August 18, 1776*," (Richmond, VA: Privately Printed, 1860), 18.

[39] Scribner and Tarter, eds., "Williamsburg City Committee, November 9, 1775," *Revolutionary Virginia: The Road to Independence*, Vol. 4, 358.

[40] Scribner and Tarter, eds., "An Introductory Note," *Revolutionary Virginia: The Road to Independence*, Vol. 5, 3.

The Committee of Safety intended to disband once the convention convened, but the amount of work involved in managing and supplying Virginia's armed forces convinced the Convention to retain the committee. It continued to meet and issue warrants for payments to a multitude of applicants.

The Convention spent the first week gathering intelligence on the situation in Virginia. Most of its attention was focused on Norfolk, where Governor Dunmore had established a base of operations. Colonel Woodford's detachment of Second Virginians and Culpeper Minutemen arrived in the region in late November and a standoff ensued about ten miles south of Norfolk at the village of Great Bridge.

Battle of Great Bridge

The Great Bridge was actually a long, narrow, manmade causeway with several wooden bridges spanning the southern branch of the Elizabeth River and its tributaries and marshland. Norfolk lay eleven miles north of the main bridge span and since most of the terrain south of Norfolk was marsh and swamp, the Great Bridge Road was the primary southern land route between Norfolk and North Carolina.

Lieutenant Colonel Charles Scott, who marched ahead of Woodford's main force with approximately 200 men, was eager to confront Dunmore's small force of "Tories and Blacks". Dunmore had removed the planks from the main bridge and built a small wooden fort on the north bank of the river adjacent to the dismantled bridge.[41] A severe shortage of ammunition limited Scott's actions, however.

---

[41] D.R. Anderson, ed., "Colonel Woodford to Edmund Pendleton, November 26, 1775," in "The Letters of Colonel William Woodford, Colonel Robert Howe, and General Charles Lee to Edmund Pendleton," *Richmond College Historical Papers*, (Richmond: VA, June, 1915) 104 and Scribner and

A few miles to the north in Norfolk, Lord Dunmore and his force of approximately 120 British regulars, a small number of Virginia Tories, and hundreds of runaway slaves who had responded to Dunmore's proclamation of freedom (issued in mid-November) to any slave of a rebel who fought for him, rushed to complete earthworks around Norfolk and prepare for Colonel Woodford's arrival. The longer Dunmore could keep Woodford's "shirtmen" (as he derisively referred to them) from crossing the dismantled bridge, the better chance he had of holding Norfolk. Lord Dunmore explained the bridge's importance to General William Howe in Boston:

> *Having heard that a thousand chosen Men belonging to the Rebels, a great part of which were Rifle men, were on their March to attack us here so to cut off our provisions, I determined to take possession of the pass at the great Bridge which Secures us the greatest part of two Counties to supply us with provisions. I accordingly ordered a Stockade Fort to be erected there, which was done in a few days, and I put an Officer and Twenty five men to Garrison it, with some Volunteers and Negroes.*[42]

While Colonel Woodford struggled in Suffolk to provide his troops with adequate ammunition, Lieutenant Colonel Scott's advance guard entrenched just south of the Great Bridge and waited for Colonel Woodford to arrive with the rest of his detachment. The bulk of Scott's force was posted behind breastworks on the southern edge of the causeway. Sentries

---

Tarter, eds., "A General Return of the Forces Under Col. Woodford at Great Bridge, December 10. 1775," *Revolutionary Virginia: The Road to Independence,* Vol. 5, 101

[42] Clark, ed., "Lord Dunmore to General William Howe, November 30, 1775," *Naval Documents of the American Revolution*, Vol. 2, 1209-11.

were posted forward of the breastworks at night, on what was essentially an island, with the Elizabeth River to the north, a small creek to the south (fifty yards in front of the "rebel" breastworks), and marsh on either side of the causeway. Hidden amongst a few buildings and piles of debris close to the dismantled bridge and Dunmore's fort, Colonel Scott's sentries were positioned to alarm their comrades at the breastworks if the enemy approached at night. For their own safety, the sentinels were withdrawn back to the breastworks at dawn each day.

Colonel Woodford, with the main body of rebel troops, reached the Great Bridge on December 2. He estimated that Dunmore's fort was defended by 250 men, most of who were escaped slaves commanded by sergeants of the Fourteenth Regiment.[43] A handful of Tories also manned the fort. Woodford speculated that it might be possible to capture it, but the presence of cannon meant that its conquest would come at a very high cost in lives. Woodford believed he held a strong position but was concerned about his limited supply of gunpowder and the lack of blankets and shoes for his men.[44]

Williamsburg Grows Anxious

Although Colonel Woodford's troops successfully engaged Dunmore's forces in a number of skirmishes around Great Bridge in early December, apprehension grew among leaders in Williamsburg that time was running out to drive Dunmore from Norfolk. Thomas Ludwell Lee of Stafford County summarized the concern of many in the Fourth Virginia Convention and Committee of Safety, both of who met daily in the capital:

---

[43]Anderson, ed., "Colonel Woodford to Edmund Pendleton December 4, 1775," *Richmond College Historical Papers*, 106.
[44] Ibid., 108-09.

> *Our Army has been for some time arrested in its march to Norfolk by a redoubt, or stockade, or hog pen, as they call it here, by way of derision, at the end of this bridge. Tho,' by the way, this hog pen seems filled with a parcel of wild-boars, which we appear not overfond to meddle with. My apprehension is that we shall be amused at this outpost, until Dunmore gets the lines at Norfolk finished; where he is now entrenching, & mounting cannon, some hundreds of negro's being employ'd in the work.*[45]

Lee's concern proved unwarranted; reinforcements from North Carolina, reportedly with cannon, were on the way.[46] In expectation of the cannon, Colonel Woodford began the construction of battery positions for the guns.[47]

Lord Dunmore soon learned that a large reinforcement of rebel troops was on their way to the Great Bridge and this news spurred him to action. He reported to Lord Dartmouth that,

> *The Rebels had procured some Cannon from North Carolina,* [which were expected to arrive any day] *and that they were also to be reinforced from Williamsburg, and knowing that our little Fort was not in a Condition to withstand anything heavier than Musquet Shot, I thought it advisable to risqué Something to save the Fort.*[48]

---

[45] Clark, ed., "Thomas Ludwell Lee to Richard Henry Lee, December 9, 1775," *Naval Documents of the American Revolution*, Vol. 3, 26-27.
[46] Clark, ed., "Lt. Col. Charles Scott to a Williamsburg Correspondent, December 4, 1775," *Naval Documents of the American Revolution*,
[47] Anderson, ed., "Colonel Woodford to Edmund Pendleton, December 4, 1775," *Richmond College Historical Papers*, 108.
[48] Clark, ed., "Lord Dunmore to Lord Dartmouth, December 13, 1775,"*Naval Documents of the American Revolution,* Vol. 3, 140-41.

Dunmore Decides to Attack

Worried that his small wooden fort would not hold against an assault by the soon to be reinforced rebels, Lord Dunmore chose to strike preemptively. In his report to Lord Dartmouth after the battle, Dunmore explained that his plan of attack called for,

> *Two Companies of Negroes to make a detour,* [cross the river] *and fall in behind the Rebels a little before break of Day in the morning, and just as Day began to break, to fall upon the rear of the Rebels, which* [Dunmore] *expected would draw their attention, and make them leave the breast work they had made near the Fort,* [Captain Leslie] *was then with the Regulars, the Volunteers and some recruits to sally out of the Fort, and attack* [the rebel] *breast work....*[49]

Dunmore hoped that the distraction caused by his black troops would allow his main force under Captain Samuel Leslie to cross the dismantled bridge and narrow causeway and storm the rebel breastworks against limited opposition. Unfortunately for Dunmore, miscommunication, or perhaps a misunderstanding of orders, prevented the diversionary attack from occurring. Dunmore noted after the battle that,

> *The Negroes by some mistake were sent out of the Fort to guard a pass, where it was thought the Rebels might attempt to pass, and where in fact some of them had Crossed a Night or two before, burnt a house or two,*

---

[49] Clark, ed., "Lord Dunmore to Lord Dartmouth, December 6 through February 18, 1776," *Naval Documents of the American Revolution*, Vol. 3, 141.

> *and returned; Captain Leslie not finding the Negroes there, imprudently Sallied out of the Fort at break of Day in the morning....* [50]

The Attack

Under cover of the dim light of dawn Captain Samuel Leslie's mixed force of approximately 350 men (redcoats, runaway slaves and Tories) advanced from their fort and hastily re-laid the bridge planks that had been removed weeks earlier.[51] If the handful of sleepy rebel pickets sheltered by the buildings on the island initially failed to notice the activity at the bridge, the discharge of the fort's cannon undoubtedly drew their attention that way. Startled at what they saw, the rebel sentries opened fire upon Dunmore's troops. One account of the battle included high praise for the sentries:

> *The conduct of our sentinels I cannot pass over in silence. Before they quitted their stations they fired at least three rounds as the enemy were crossing the bridge, and one of them, who was posted behind some shingles, kept his ground till he had fired eight times, and after receiving a whole platoon, made his escape over the causeway into our breast works.*[52]

As the sentinels scurried back to the rebel earthworks approximately 300 yards to the rear, their comrades behind the

---

[50] Ibid.
Note: Lord Dunmore claimed in this letter that he left the discretion of whether to actually launch the attack with Captain Leslie.
[51] Clark, ed., "Letter to John Pinkney, December 20, 1775," *Naval Documents of the American Revolution*, Vol. 3, 186-89.
[52] Ibid.
Note: The brave sentinel who stood his ground for so long was twenty year old Billy Flora, a free born black volunteer from Norfolk.

breastwork began to stir, realizing that the gunfire they heard was not the normal morning salute of the past few days.

Four hundred yards south of the earthworks in the main rebel encampment, however, few of Colonel Woodford's troops (who had just awakened to reveille) took notice of the distant gunfire. Major Alexander Spotswood recalled

> *We were alarmed this morning by the firing of some guns after reveille beating, which, as the enemy had paid us this compliment several times before, we at first concluded to be nothing but a morning salute.*[53]

Colonel Woodford had a similar reaction:

> *After reveille beating, two or three great guns, and some musquetry were discharged from the enemy's fort, which, as it was not an unusual thing, was but little regarded.*[54]

The situation was much different at the rebel breastworks. Realizing that they were under attack, the commander of the guard, Lieutenant Edward Travis, ordered his small detachment of approximately sixty men, "*to reserve their fire till the enemy came within the distance of fifty yards.*"[55] To their front across a narrow 200 yard causeway were more than five times their number of enemy troops with two cannon that, "*played briskly,*" upon the Virginians defending the breastwork.[56]

---

[53] Peter Force, ed., "Major Spotswood to a Friend in Williamsburgh, December 9, 1775," *American Archives*, Vol. 4, 224.

[54] Clark, ed., "Col. Woodford to Edmund Pendleton, December 10, 1775," *Naval Documents of the American Revolution,* Vol. 3, 39-40.

[55] Force, ed., "Major Spotswood to a Friend in Williamsburgh, December 9, 1775," *American Archives*, Vol. 4, 224 and Clark, ed. "Letter to Pinkney, December 20, 1775", *Naval Documents of the American Revolution*, Vol. 3, 186-89.

[56] Clark, ed., "Letter to Pinkney, December 20, 1775," *Naval Documents of the American Revolution*, Vol. 3, 186-89.

Joining the British cannon at the edge of the island were the Tory and black soldiers of Dunmore, over 200 strong. Behind them rose the smoke of several buildings – formerly the outposts of the rebel sentries but now torched by Dunmore's troops. Captain Leslie remained on the island with the Tory and black troops while Captain Charles Fordyce led the British regulars of the Fourteenth Regiment, over one hundred strong, in a column six abreast across the narrow causeway to storm the rebel earthworks.[57]

Back in the main "rebel" camp, the gravity of the situation had finally become apparent. Major Spotswood recalled

> *I heard Adjutant Blackburn call out, Boys! Stand to your arms! Colonel Woodford and myself immediately got equipped, and ran out; the Colonel pressed down to the breastwork in our front, and my alarm-post being two hundred and fifty yards in another quarter, I ran to it as fast as I could, and by the time I had made all ready for engaging, a very heavy fire ensued at the breastwork, in which were not more than sixty men.*[58]

The heavy fire that Major Spotswood heard came from Lieutenant Travis's guard detail and a few brave reinforcements who had rushed forward at the first alarm.

The valor of some of the rebels was acknowledged by Major Spotswood, who proudly noted in a letter immediately after the engagement that as the redcoats approached the breastworks with fixed bayonets, "*Our young troops received them with firmness, and behaved as well as it was possible for*

---

[57] Clark, ed., "Letter from a Midshipman on Board H.M. Sloop Otter, December 9, 1775" *Naval Documents of the American Revolution*, Vol. 3, 29.

[58] Force, ed., "Major Spotswood to a Friend in Williamsburgh, December 9, 1775," *American Archives*, Vol. 4, 224.

soldiers to do."[59] In his own letter after the battle, Colonel Woodford also commented on the rebel fire from the breastwork, writing that, "*perhaps a hotter fire never happened, or a greater carnage, for the number of troops.*"[60]

The hot fire delivered upon the British originated not only from the breastworks directly in front of them, but also from breastworks on high ground west of the causeway. Riflemen from the Culpeper Minute Battalion manned this position and poured deadly enfilade fire into the British column's right flank.[61] According to one American account, the intense rebel small arms fire from both positions

> *Threw* [the advancing British regulars] *into some confusion, but they were instantly rallied by a Captain Fordyce, and advanced along the causeway with great resolution, keeping up a constant and heavy fire as they approached. The brave Fordyce exerted himself to keep up their spirits, reminded them of their ancient glory, and waving his hat over his head, encouragingly told them the day was their own. Thus pressing forward, he fell within fifteen steps to the breast-work. His wounds were many, and his death would have been that of a hero, had he met it in a better cause.*[62]

Captain Fordyce, riddled with over a dozen wounds, was one of many redcoats to fall before the American earthworks. Strewn about the ground just a few paces from the Virginians

---

[59] Ibid.

[60] Clark, ed., "Col. Woodford to Edmund Pendleton, December 10, 1775,"*Naval Documents of the American Revolution,* Vol. 3, 39-49.

[61] *The Annual Register for the Year 1776*, 4th ed. 29.

[62] Clark, "Letter to Pinkney, December 20, 1775", *Naval Documents of the American Revolution*, Vol. 3, 186-89.

were over thirty British dead and wounded. One rebel officer described a scene of bloody carnage before the breastworks:

> *The scene, when the dead and wounded were bro't off, was too much; I then saw the horrors of war in perfection, worse than can be imagin'd; 10 and 12 bullets thro' many; limbs broke in 2 or 3 places; brains turning out. Good God, what a sight!*[63]

Captain Fordyce and twelve British privates lay dead in front of the breastworks and nearly a score of wounded redcoats, including Lieutenant John Batut, who led the British advance guard, were taken prisoner. An American observer noted that

> *The progress of the enemy was now at an end;* [the survivors] *retreated over the causeway with precipitation, and were dreadfully galled in their rear. Hitherto, on our side only the guard, consisting of twenty five, and some others, upon the whole, amounting to not more than ninety, had been engaged. Only the regulars of the 14th regiment, in number one hundred and twenty, had advanced upon the causeway, and about two hundred and thirty tories and negroes had, after crossing the bridge, continued upon the island.*[64]

The British made a stand upon the island between the fort and rebel earthworks, but according to an eyewitness, it was brief and they,

---

[63] Charles Campbell, ed., "Richard Kidder Meade to Theodorick Bland Jr., December 18, 1775" *The Bland Papers*, Vol. 1, (1840), 38-39.
[64] Clark, "Letter to Pinkney, December 20, 1775," *Naval Documents of the American Revolution*, Vol. 3, 186-89.

> *Fled into their fort, leaving behind them the two field pieces, which, however, they took care to spike up with nails. Many were killed and wounded in the flight, but colonel Woodford very prudently restrained his troops from urging their pursuit too far. From the beginning of the attack till the repulse from the breast work might be about fourteen or fifteen minutes; till the total defeat upwards of half an hour. It is said that some of the enemy preferred death to captivity, from fear of being scalped, which lord Dunmore inhumanly told them would be their fate should they be taken alive. Thirty one, killed and wounded, fell into our hands, and the number borne off was much greater.* [65]

Aftermath

The Battle of Great Bridge was a decisive victory for the Virginians. Colonel Woodford proudly described it as, "*a second Bunker's Hill affair, in miniature; with this difference, that we kept our post, and had only one man wounded in the hand.*"[66] More than one observer attributed the lack of rebel casualties to providence (divine intervention). The British Fourteenth Regiment of Foot, on the other hand, was shattered in the attack. Their bold assault on the rebel breastworks cost them half their men. Lord Dunmore reported 3 officers and 17 men were killed and 1 officer and 43 men wounded.[67] The number of casualties among Dunmore's Tory and black soldiers is unknown.

---

[65] Ibid.

[66] Clark, ed., "Colonel Woodford to Edmund Pendleton, December 10, 1775," *Naval Documents of the American Revolution*, Vol. 3, 39-40.

[67] Clark, ed., "Lord Dunmore to Lord Dartmouth, December 13, 1775" *Naval Documents of the American Revolution*, Vol. 3, 141.

Calm settled over the causeway after the battle as Colonel Woodford dispatched an officer under a flag of truce to allow Captain Leslie to collect his dead and wounded from the battlefield.[68] With both sides safely secured behind their fortifications, the sun set with no more fighting.[69]

Fourteenth Regiment's heavy losses apparently had a strong impact on Captain Leslie. The Virginia Committee of Safety in Williamsburg gleefully reported a few days after the battle that,

> *The Regulars, disgusted, refused to fight in junction with Blacks; and Captain Leslie, we are told, declared no more of his troops should be sacrificed to whims, and put them on board the ships, in consequence of which Norfolk is abandoned, and we expect is now occupied by our troops, who were on their march there when our last account was dispatched. Many Tories are come to us, and their cases now under consideration. More notorious ones are gone on board the vessels, which have in them very valuable cargoes.*[70]

The Fourth Virginia Convention

The news of Lord Dunmore's stunning defeat at the Great Bridge was well received in Williamsburg. The Convention unanimously expressed its approval of Colonel Woodford's success as well as his humane treatment of the many wounded

---

[68] Clark, ed., "Colonel Woodford to Edmund Pendleton, December 9, 1775," *Naval Documents of the American Revolution*, Vol. 3, 28.
[69] Clark, ed., "Lord Dunmore to Lord Dartmouth, December 13, 1775," *Naval Documents of the American Revolution,* Vol. 3, 140-41.
[70] Clark, ed., "Letter from the Virginia Committee of Safety, December 16, 1775," *Naval Documents of the American Revolution*, Vol. 3, 132.

prisoners in his possession.[71] The following day, (December 13,) the convention voted to increase the size of Virginia's regular forces from two regiments to nine.[72] Each regiment was to consist of ten companies of 68 rank and file. Company officers, sergeants, musicians, and regimental officers and staff, put the total number of soldiers in each regiment above 700 men each.[73] It was a significant escalation of military preparedness that placed Virginia, and Williamsburg, on a full wartime footing.

The expense of this escalation was eased somewhat for Virginia when the Continental Congress voted to place six Virginia regiments upon continental establishment.[74] This meant that Congress and General Washington would have authority over the regiments instead of the Virginia Convention or Committee of Safety. It also meant that Congress assumed responsibility for much of the cost of the regiments, a responsibility they struggled to meet during the entire war.

Virginia's leaders appealed to Congress to add the three remaining regiments being raised in Virginia, the Seventh, Eighth, and Nineth regiments, to continental service, but the representatives in Philadelphia balked at this. They changed their mind in the spring, however, upon reports of a possible British military expedition in the southern colonies.

The readiness of these new troops was still months away. They first had to be raised in their counties. While this occurred

---

[71] Scribner and Tarter, eds., "Proceedings of the Eighth day of the 4th Virginia Convention, December 12, 1775," *Revolutionary Virginia: The Road to Independence,* Vol. 5, 114-115.
[72] Scribner and Tarter, eds., "Proceedings of the Ninth day of the 4th Virginia Convention, December 13, 1775," *Revolutionary Virginia: The Road to Independence,* Vol. 5, 128.
[73] Ibid.
[74] Ford, ed., "Proceedings of the Continental Congress, December 28, 1775," *Journals of the Continental Congress*, Vol. 3, 463.

over the winter, Colonel Woodford, who was reinforced by three of Colonel Henry's companies, remained on the south side of the James River. They occupied Norfolk, which Lord Dunmore abandoned after his defeat at Great Bridge, and burned it to the ground in early January during a skirmish with Dunmore's ships. Woodford's troops then spent the winter in Suffolk, ready to react if Dunmore and his few supporters dared come ashore, but they did not and spent most of the winter aboard an assortment of ships anchored in the Elizabeth River.

In Williamsburg, the remnants of Colonel Henry's First Virginia, (who were not attached to Colonel Woodford or posted in Hampton) and Captain Robert Anderson's company of Williamsburg minutemen, remained in the capital. With Dunmore seemingly contained, the Committee of Safety discharged Anderson's minutemen just before Christmas, expecting a minute battalion from the Prince William District to arrive any day.[75]

It appears the militia from northern Virginia were either delayed on their march or sent on to Hampton, for in early January a report of British warships in the York River alarmed the capital, but there were few troops available to send to Yorktown. Colonel Henry sent one company of riflemen from his regiment to reinforce Yorktown's defenders (likely York County militia). Purdie's *Virginia Gazette* reported that, "*Many gentlemen volunteers likewise went from this city, to assist their brethren in York; and our worthy delegates formed themselves under the old intrepid warrior, Col. Andrew Lewis, for the protection of the city.*"[76] These preparations proved

---

[75] Scribner and Tarter, eds., "Instructions to Colonel Henry from the Committee of Safety, December 23, 1775" and "Edmund Pendleton to Colonel Henry, December 23, 1775," *Revolutionary Virginia: The Road to Independence,* Vol. 5, 230, 229.

[76] Purdie, "Williamsburg, January 5, 1776," *Virginia Gazette*, 3.

unnecessary when it was discovered that the ships were not hostile.

With the expansion of Virginia's regular forces from two regiments to nine, county committees throughout Virginia scrambled to raise additional troops committed to two years of service. There simply were not enough men available to fill the new regiments and maintain the minute battalions, so Virginia's minutemen were largely dissolved by the spring of 1776.

Four

1776

Building Virginia's new military establishment was the primary task of the Fourth Virginia Convention at the start of 1776. Before it became too embroiled in that, however, the Convention appointed a new Committee of Safety for the upcoming year. What had initially been a committee to govern the colony when the conventions were not in session had become a vital part of the government in its own right. Nine of the eleven original members were retained on the committee. George Mason, whose ill health kept him at home in Fairfax County, and Carter Braxton, who was selected by the Convention to serve in the Continental Congress in place of Peyton Randolph, who died in Philadelphia in October, were the only two members who did not return to the committee.[1] The committee continued to tackle the logistical challenges of supplying Virginia's armed forces while the convention focused on forming the new regiments.

It took the Convention until mid-January to finalize the appointment of regimental officers in Virginia's new regular forces. The assembly wrapped up its business on January 20, and handed the responsibility of further governance to the Committee of Safety. Just as before, the committee took up the monumental challenge of forming yet another new military establishment, one that was four times larger than the previous one. Paying for the recruitment, provision and supplies for this

---

[1] Scribner and Tarter, eds., "Proceedings of the Twelfth day of the 4th Virginia Convention, December 16, 1775," *Revolutionary Virginia: The Road to Independence,* Vol. 5, 158.

force was a daunting task and the committee scrutinized and approved most expenditures.

The impact upon Williamsburg of such a large military force was not as great as one might expect. The Committee of Safety resolved in mid-February to station the newly raised regiments along the major rivers of Virginia. As a result, only two regiments, Colonel Henry's First Virginia and the newly formed Sixth Virginia Regiment, were initially posted in Williamsburg to guard the York and James Rivers.[2]

Colonel Henry's First Virginia was scattered in three locations, Williamsburg, Suffolk and Hampton. Henry had become frustrated by the lack of respect shown him by both Colonel Woodford and the Committee of Safety and the final straw for him occurred in late February when he learned that the Continental Congress had not promoted him to the rank of brigadier-general with over all command of Virginia's regular forces.

This insult, for which he blamed the Committee of Safety, prompted Henry to resign his commission in protest. His resignation was accepted by the committee (who had doubts about his military abilities from the start) but not by Henry's officers and men. A near mutiny developed among the troops in Williamsburg when word of Henry's resignation was revealed. The troops went into, "*deep mourning*" and gathered, under arms at Henry's lodging in Williamsburg to address him.[3]

Henry graciously thanked those assembled for their support and then attended a farewell dinner in his honor at the Raleigh Tavern with his officers. He was forced to postpone his departure from the capital, however, when word spread of,

---

[2] Scribner and Tarter, eds., "Proceedings of the Virginia Committee of Safety, February 10, 1776," *Revolutionary Virginia: The Road to Independence,* Vol. 6, 85.

[3] Purdie, "March 1, 1776," *Virginia Gazette*, 3.

"*some uneasiness getting among the soldiery, who assembled in a tumultuous manner, and demanded their discharge, declaring their unwillingness to serve under any other commander.*"[4] Henry spent most of the evening with the troops, "*visiting the several barracks, and* [using] *every argument in his power with the soldiery to lay aside their imprudent resolution, and continue in the service…*"[5] His efforts succeeded and the disgruntled troops eventually settled down.

Although most of the newly raised troops in Virginia were stationed at posts other than Williamsburg, the regimental officers of each regiment regularly rode to Williamsburg to accept the commissions. This is what brought Colonel Hugh Mercer to the capital in early March.

Colonel Mercer commanded the Third Virginia Regiment and had very nearly been appointed commander of the First Virginia instead of Patrick Henry back in August of 1775. Concern among many delegates at the Third Convention about Henry's qualifications and lack of military experience had prompted a significant number of members to support Mercer (who had extensive military experience from the French and Indian War). Alas, Henry's popularity won the day and Mercer returned to Fredericksburg in the fall of 1775 to command a minute battalion.

Although the troops in Williamsburg were not a part of Mercer's Third regiment, Colonel Henry's resignation from the army and Colonel Woodford absence (he had gone home to Caroline County on leave) left Mercer the ranking officer in Williamsburg. Likely disturbed at a lack of order and discipline among the troops there, he set out to address this concern not only with Henry's First Regiment, but also a

---

[4] Ibid.
[5] Ibid.

portion of the Sixth Virginia Regiment, which began arriving in Williamsburg in March.

Colonel Mercer declared in his general orders that officers were answerable for any disturbance of the peace in town caused by their men and instructed company officers to frequently inspect the quarters of the troops for damage and cleanliness.[6] Officers were also instructed to exercise their men more to enhance discipline while the troops were reminded that,

> *Every Soldier is to Consider himself as intended to Protect the inhabitants of this Country* [so] *if contrary to this intention* [a soldier] *should insult or* injure [the inhabitants] *in their persons or property, he may Depend on being Treated with Severity.*[7]

Edmund Pendleton acknowledged Mercer's progress with the troops but also noted some resistance to his efforts:

> *Colonel Mercer has done great things towards a Reform which has given great pleasure to the Judicious, but I understand has produced a Court of Enquiry into his Conduct….*[8]

---

[6] R. A. Brock, ed., "General Orders, March, 5 and 7, The Orderly Book of the Company of Captain George Stubblefield, Fifth Virginia Regiment, from March 3 to July 10, 1776," *Collections of the Virginia Historical Society*, New Series, Vol. 6, (Richmond, VA: 1888), 145-147.

[7] Brock, ed., "General Orders March 7 and 11, 1776," The Orderly Book of the Company of Captain George Stubblefield, Fifth Virginia Regiment, from March 3 to July 10, 1776," *Collections of the Virginia Historical Society*, New Series, Vol. 6, 147, 149-150.

[8] David John Mays, ed., "To William Woodford, 16 March, 1776," *The Letters and Papers of Edmund Pendleton, 1734-1803,* Vol. 1, (Charlottesville, VA: University Press of Virginia, 1967,) 158-159.

Mutiny of Gibson's Lambs

The specific incident that sparked an inquiry into Mercer's conduct involved Captain George Gibson's company of Augusta County riflemen in the First Virginia. Captain Gibson was absent so his ranking lieutenant, William Lynn, commanded the rifle company. These frontier riflemen from Augusta County, who became known sarcastically as Gibson's lambs, bristled at Mercer's efforts to reign in their behavior. When two of them were lightly punished by a court martial for behavior that Colonel Mercer believed was "seditious", he disapproved of the sentence and had them placed in irons until Brigadier-General Robert Howe of North Carolina arrived to take up the matter.[9]

If that had been all Mercer did, the matter might have ended there, but Colonel Mercer was determined to end the rampant defiance to military authority in Gibson's company and took the additional step of disarming the rest of Gibson's riflemen for the, "*Same Seditious and Mutinous Spirit,*" and placed them all on fatigue duty (work detail) under guard. The captain of the guard was instructed that,

> *If any of these Seditious and Mutinous Soldiers Shall dare to Refuse to Perform the Duty which the Quarter-Master Shall direct, such offenders shall be put in Irons...* [and] *if any obstruction arise from the same Mutinous Disposition, the Guard is to fire on the offenders With such Effect as to kill them if possible.*[10]

Mercer's harsh directive was successful in containing the defiant troops, but his threat to shoot any offender of his orders

---

[9] Brock, ed., "After Orders, March 11, 1776, The Orderly Book of the Company of Captain George Stubblefield, Fifth Virginia Regiment...." *Collections of the Virginia Historical Society*, New Series, Vol. 6, 150-151.
[10] Ibid.

was challenged by the officers of Gibson's company as too extreme, and they appealed to General Howe of North Carolina when he arrived in Williamsburg in mid-March. The result was an apology from Colonel Mercer posted in the general orders of March 17:

> *Head-Quarters, March 17, 1776*
> *General Orders -- Col. Mercer, sensible that he exceeded the line of duty in his treatment of capt. Gibson's company, has requested the commanding-officer to declare, in orders, that he had no personal intention in any thing he did, and in this publick manner desires to acknowledge he was wrong, and assures the company he is sorry for what happened. The commanding officer is of opinion, that this officer-like acknowledgement of the colonel's ought to be satisfactory to the company.*[11]

Lieutenant Lynn of Gibson's company, responding to negative reports and rumors about the conduct of his company, sent a copy of Mercer's comments to the gazettes, which published it in early April.[12] An angry Colonel Mercer, who had returned to northern Virginia to command the Third Regiment, replied to Lynn with his own letter to the gazettes. He asserted that his actions towards Gibson's company were for the good of both Gibson's men (who lacked sufficient discipline) and the army in general. He also placed blame for the incident upon Lieutenant Lynn and his fellow officers who, Mercer contended, had neglected to adequately discipline their troops in the months leading up to the incident and had thus helped create the mutinous spirit of the men.

---

[11] Purdie, "April 5, 1776," *Virginia Gazette*, 3.
[12] Ibid.

Fredericksburg, April 10, 1776
The publick, to whom lieut. Lynn thought proper to report an affair of military discipline, will naturally conclude from his publication that I have injured the characters of the men of capt. Gibson's company of regulars. I aimed at mending the character of that company, and hope I have not missed my aim. In attempting this necessary service, it is true, some deviation was made from the line of duty; but whose deviation from duty was most injurious to that company, and to the cause in which we are engaged, I beg leave also to submit to the publick: That of an officer who quells a mutinous spirit in the troops, or of those officers who, by a neglect of discipline, had, after some months training, obliged me to take the trouble of reducing their men to some degree of military order.[13]

General Charles Lee Arrives

Reports of a planned British expedition in the South prompted the Continental Congress to order Major-General Charles Lee to proceed from New York City, where he had been sent at the start of 1776 to organize the city's defenses, to the South, where his military expertise was needed. A former British officer with extensive military experience in Europe, Lee served with General Washington in Boston in 1775. Although he was a native of Britain and had only arrived in the colonies in 1773, Lee earned the trust and admiration of many in Congress and held the third-highest rank in the Continental

---

[13] Purdie, "April 19, 1776," *Virginia Gazette*, 4.

Army. He was the most experienced and knowledgeable officer in the army and was highly esteemed throughout the colonies.

Lee's arrival in Williamsburg in late March was welcomed by Virginia's leaders. He reported to General Washington that, "*The Regiments in general are very compleat in numbers of Men (those that I have seen) fine—but a most horrid deficiency of Arms – no entrenching tools, no guns* [cannon]…. *I have order'd…the Artificers to work night and day.*"[14]

Lee was particularly critical of the scattered deployment of Virginia's regiments. The Committee of Safety in February had dispersed the regiments throughout the tidewater region, leaving the Nineth Virginia on the Eastern shore and placing two regiments each upon Virginia's three peninsulas and the southside of the James River. The committee explained to General Lee that this was done to protect each region and make it easier to provision the troops.[15]

General Lee disagreed with the deployment and ordered the Third and Fifth Virginia Regiments to march to Williamsburg.[16] When he learned that Congress had placed the Seventh, Eighth, and Nineth Virginia Regiments under Continental (and thus his authority), Lee ordered the Third Virginia to remain along the Potomac River and the Seventh Virginia, posted closer to the capital in Gloucester County, to march to Williamsburg instead.[17]

---

[14] Lee, "General Lee to General Washington, April 5, 1776," *The Lee Papers*, Vol. 1, 376-377.

[15] Scribner and Tarter, eds., "John Page to General Charles Lee, April 10, 1776,"," *Revolutionary Virginia: The Road to Independence,* Vol. 6, 371-372.

[16] Charles Lee, "General Lee to Colonels Peachy and Mercer, April 2, 1776," *The Lee Papers*, Vol. 1, 369.

[17] Lee, "General Lee to General Mercer, April 10, 1776," *The Lee Papers*, Vol. 1, 409.

Leaders in Gloucester appealed to the Committee of Safety to keep the Seventh Virginia in Gloucester. A compromise was struck; half of the regiment marched to the capital in the end of April and the remainder stayed in Gloucester County.[18] The Fifth Virginia's stay in Williamsburg was also altered, it was sent across the James River to Suffolk in anticipation of a possible march into the Carolina's.[19] That left the Sixth Virginia, part of the First Virginia, and half of the Seventh Virginia, approximately 1,400 men, posted in Williamsburg and Hampton.[20] Stray companies from other regiments as well as officers seeking their commissions also passed through and sometimes lingered in Williamsburg in April on their way to join their assigned regiments.[21]

Measures were taken to prevent the troops from getting into mischief, both in camp and in the city. Gaming (gambling) was strictly prohibited but not necessarily strictly enforced, and the troops were instructed that they should spend whatever leisure time they had on, "*improving* [themselves] *in the Military service.*"[22]

---

[18] Thomas Posey, "Journal Entry, April 30, 1776," *Revolutionary War Journal, Thomas Posey Papers,* Indiana Historical Society Library, Indianapolis, IN.

[19] Brock, ed., "April 13-14, 21, 1776, Orderly Book of Captain George Stubblefield, Fifth Virginia Regiment...," *Miscellaneous Papers...in the Collections of the Virginia Historical Society*, 162-163.

[20] Note: This is an estimate based on General Lee's observation that the troop strength of the Virginia regiments in April 1776 were near complete. If so, the 6th Virginia would account for over 700 men, the 1st, likely less due to their longer service (attrition) and detachment in Hampton likely had approximately 300 men, and half of the 7th Virginia, approximately 350 officers and men.

[21] Campbell, ed., "After Orders, April 4, 1776 and General Orders, April 5, 1776 and General Orders, April 10, 1776," *The Orderly Book of the Portion of the American Army Stationed at or Near Williamsburg...,* 15-16, 20.

[22] Campbell, ed., "General Orders, March 23, 1776," *The Orderly Book of the Portion of the American Army Stationed at or Near Williamsburg...,* 4.

The troops were frequently paraded for roll call, drill and sometimes review, and while it is unclear where their parade ground was in the spring of 1776, occasional orders to form on the green before the palace, or parade by the Capitol, suggests that both open areas were used by the troops in addition to a main parade ground.[23] The troops also assembled regularly at Waller's Grove, near the capitol, to attend church service.[24]

A visitor to Williamsburg in the spring of 1776 likely would have witnessed over the course of the day soldiers paraded for roll call or drill, musicians gathered to practice the fife and drum (at a specified time and location so as not to confuse the troops whose orders were often conveyed through music) and officers scurrying about town to arrange for clothing and gear for their men. There were also fatigue (work) parties busy in camp and about the city and guard detachments that marched out of or returned to Williamsburg from posts on the James and York rivers.

It was also, of course, a busy time for the city's tradesmen, many who were overwhelmed with orders and plagued with material shortages. Blacksmiths, gunsmiths, tinsmiths, carpenters, coopers, and tailors were just some of the trades kept busy by the army's presence in Williamsburg.

General Andrew Lewis, a veteran of both the French and Indian War and Dunmore's recent expedition against the Shawnee Indians, arrived in Williamsburg in late March to receive his brigadier's commission granted by the Continental Congress.[25] When General Lee travelled to Suffolk in mid-

---

[23] Campbell, ed., "General Orders, April 2, 1776 and April 8, 1776," *The Orderly Book of the Portion of the American Army Stationed at or Near Williamsburg...,* 12, 18.
[24] Campbell, ed., "General Orders, March 24, 1776 and April 19, 1776," *The Orderly Book of the Portion of the American Army Stationed at or Near Williamsburg...,* 5, 27.
[25] Purdie, "Williamsburg, April 5, 1776," *Virginia Gazette,* 3.

April to inspect the situation south of the James River, Lewis assumed command of the troops in Williamsburg. Lee instructed Lewis to, "*clear the college for a hospital,*" and prepare it to receive all the sick troops presently in Suffolk.[26] Although the Committee of Safety approved Lee's decision to use the college as a hospital, they complained to him that his unilateral action, without any consultation with the committee, was an, "*improper step* [that they presumed was] *preceded by inattention.*"[27]

This was not the first time General Lee annoyed the Committee of Safety nor they him. Lee complained to General Washington within a week of his arrival in Williamsburg of his frustration with the Committee of Safety.

> *I am sorry to grate your ears with a truth, but must at all events assure you that the Provincial Congress of New York are angels of decision when compared to your countrymen – the Committee of Safety assembled in Williamsburgh. Page, Lee, Mercer, and Payne are indeed exceptions, but from Pendleton, Bland, the Treasurer & Co., libera nos Domine!* [Lord Deliver Us].[28]

Lee expressed a similar frustration to Richard Henry Lee, who was with the Congress in Philadelphia, writing that, "*the namby*

---

[26] Lee, "General Lee to John Page, April 21, 1776," *The Lee Papers*, Vol. 1, 437.
[27] Mays, ed., "Edmund Pendleton to Charles Lee, April 25, 1776," *The Letters and Papers of Edmund Pendleton, 1734-1803*, Vol. 1, 165.
[28] Lee, "General Lee to General Washington, April 5, 1776," *The Lee Papers*, Vol. 1, 376-378.

pamby's of the senatorial part of the continent...grow more timid and hysterical."[29]

General Lee's stay in Virginia, however, proved brief. By mid-May he was on the march with the Eighth Virginia Regiment to North Carolina and ultimately Charleston, South Carolina, arriving in time to participate in the Battle of Sullivan's Island to repulse a British attack upon Charleston. General Lewis assumed command of the troops in Virginia.

Independence

The attention of many Virginians swung from military affairs to political affairs in May when the fifth and final Virginia Convention gathered in Williamsburg to address what was on everyone's mind, independence. The delegates selected Edmund Pendleton to chair the convention and spent a week on routine matters such as committee work and petitions from constituents.

On May 14, the Convention addressed the issue at hand, independence. It was presented in three competing resolutions. After a full day of debate, Patrick Henry's resolution, which was the most comprehensive of the three, became the basis for a compromise. On May 15, this new compromise resolution, which listed the colonists' grievances against Great Britain and instructed Virginia's delegates at the Continental Congress in Philadelphia to, "*Propose to that respectable body to declare the United Colonies free and independent upon the crown and parliament of Great Britain...*," was approved unanimously by the Fifth Virginia Convention."[30]

---

[29] Lee, "General Lee to Richard Henry Lee, April 5, 1776, *The Lee Papers,* Vol. 1, 378-379.
[30] Brent Tarter, ed., "Proceedings of the Ninth Day of the Virginia Convention, May 15, 1776," *Revolutionary Virginia: Road to Independence,* Vol. 7, Part 1, (University Press of Virginia, 1983), 143.

The Convention then formed a committee tasked with drafting a Declaration of Rights and a new plan for Virginia's government to replace the defunct royal government.[31]

Recognizing the significance of their vote, the Convention cut its deliberation short the following day to celebrate with the soldiers and inhabitants of Williamsburg. Purdie's *Virginia Gazette* described the celebration.

> *In consequence of...the resolution, universally regarded as the only door which will lead to safety and prosperity, some gentlemen made a handsome collection for the purpose of treating the soldiery, who next day were paraded in Waller's grove, before brigadier-general Lewis, attended by the gentlemen of the Committee of Safety, the members of the General Convention, the inhabitants of this city, &c, &c. The resolution being read aloud to the army, the following toasts were given, each of them accompanied by a discharge of the artillery and small arms, and the acclamations of all present:*
>
> *The American independent states*
> *The Grand Congress of the United States, and their respective legislatures*
> *General Washington and victory to American arms.*
>
> *The UNION FLAG of the American states waved upon the Capitol during the whole of this ceremony, which being ended, the soldiers partook of the refreshment prepared for them by the affection of their countrymen, and the evening concluded with illuminations, and*

---

[31] Ibid.

> *other demonstrations of joy, every one seeming pleased that the dominion of Great Britain was now at an end....*[32]

With the business of war demanding attention, the Committee of Safety met before and after the celebration on May 16.[33] The committee met the next day as well, despite the Convention's proclamation a week earlier that May 17 was to be a day of fasting, humiliation, and prayer.[34] The Convention did not meet nor the troops drill, but they did attend divine service, probably in Waller's Grove.[35]

It was business as usual for the Convention, Committee of Safety, and troops by Saturday May 18. The Convention addressed numerous petitions from Virginians while the committee appointed to prepare a Declaration of Rights and a new form of government worked towards those goals. The Committee of Safety continued to grant warrants to pay for the war and the troops in Williamsburg continued to drill. Even the college of William and Mary prepared to return to normal, announcing that the building briefly used as a hospital had been cleaned and would be plastered and whitewashed in preparation for a resumption of classes in June.[36]

On May 24, a portion of the army marched out of Williamsburg and established a new camp at Great Spring. This was possibly in response to a report that arrived a day earlier

---

[32] Purdie, "May 17, 1776," *Virginia Gazette,* 3.

[33] Tarter, ed., "Proceedings of the Virginia Committee of Safety, May 16, 1776," *Revolutionary Virginia: Road to Independence*, Vol. 7, Part 1, 168-170.

[34] Tarter, ed., "Proceedings of the Virginia Committee of Safety, May 17, 1776," *Revolutionary Virginia: Road to Independence*, Vol. 7, Part 1, 174-175.

[35] Campbell, ed., "General Orders, May 17, 1776," *The Orderly Book of the Portion of the American Army Stationed at or Near Williamsburg....*, 39.

[36] Purdie, "May 24, 1776," *Virginia Gazette*, 4.

that Lord Dunmore and his fleet had sailed from Portsmouth into the James River.[37] An unknown number of troops from the First and Sixth Regiments as well as some from the recently arrived Second Virginia Regiment encamped at Great Spring. It appears that this camp was a secondary camp, perhaps for just a detachment, because the highest ranking officers listed in an orderly book that still exist were captains.[38] In Williamsburg, colonels, lieutenant colonels, and majors were typically appointed officer of the day in the daily orders, but no such officer appears in the orderly book at the Great Spring camp, the location of which remains a mystery.

Shocking news of Lord Dunmore's arrival at Gwynn's Island in the Chesapeake Bay reached Williamsburg on May 27, and alarmed the city. General Lewis ordered the five companies of the Seventh Virginia in Williamsburg (half the regiment) to re-join the rest of their regiment in Gloucester County.[39] The Seventh Virginia was the closest continental unit to Gwynn's Island and its troops marched to the eastern end of Gloucester County (today Mathews County) to challenge and hopefully contain Lord Dunmore and his supporters. A six-week stalemate ensued as both sides built earthworks.

The Third Virginia Regiment, which was still posted on the Potomac River in Alexandria and Dumfries, was also ordered to march to Williamsburg in response to Dunmore's occupation of Gwynn's Island.[40] A portion of the regiment arrived in the

---

[37] Campbell, ed., "General Orders, May 24, 1776," *The Orderly Book of the Portion of the American Army Stationed at or Near Williamsburg….*, 41, and Lee, "General Lewis to General Lee, May 27, 1776, *The Lee Papers,* Vol. 2, 42.

[38] Campbell, ed., "General Orders, May 23-27, 1776," *The Orderly Book of the Portion of the American Army Stationed at or Near Williamsburg….*, 40-42.

[39] Lee, "General Lewis to General Lee, May 27, 1776, *The Lee Papers,* Vol. 2, 43.

[40] Ibid.

capital by early June and by late June the influx of soldiers from the Third Virginia as well as the rest of the Second and the Fourth Virginia, which had been ordered to Williamsburg from Suffolk, required the establishment of another camp.[41] One had already been established in early June outside of Williamsburg, (called Spring Field) likely as a post to defend against the possible approach of the enemy from the York River.[42] Another camp was established within Williamsburg in late June on the, "*Green near the college*."[43] It was probably established where the old camp had been behind the Wren building, but it is possible that site was no longer useable and the college camp in 1776 was erected on the green in the front of the building. Yet another camp, (Deep Spring) was established by early August, its location, like the camps at Great Spring, and Spring Field, remain uncertain.[44]

While troops converged on both Williamsburg and Gloucester County, Virginia's political leaders in the capitol hammered out a Declaration of Rights and a new constitution. The Declaration of Rights was completed on June 12 and the constitution on June 29. Patrick Henry was elected as the commonwealth of Virginia's first governor and invited to assume residence of the Governor's palace, which undoubtedly needed repair to accommodate Governor Henry and his

---

[41] Ibid.
[42] Campbell, ed., "General Orders, June 5, 1776," *The Orderly Book of the Portion of the American Army Stationed at or Near Williamsburg….*, 46.
[43] Campbell, ed., "General Orders, June 8, and June 28, 1776," *The Orderly Book of the Portion of the American Army Stationed at or Near Williamsburg….*, 47-48, 57, and Lee, "General Lewis to General Lee, June 12, 1776, *The Lee Papers*, Vol. 2, 62-64.
[44] Campbell, ed., "General Orders, August 2, 1776," *The Orderly Book of the Portion of the American Army Stationed at or Near Williamsburg….*, 67. Note: The location of the camps at Great Spring, Spring Field, and Deep Spring remain uncertain, but were certainly just outside of Williamsburg.

family.[45] On the last day of its session, the Convention authorized an expenditure of up to $1,000 (pounds) to provide furniture for the governor's residence.[46]

With the adjournment of the Convention and Committee of Safety on July 5, governing authority passed to Governor Henry and his Council of State, to be joined in a few months by the new state legislature, made up of a House of Delegates and Senate, once members were elected over the summer.

Gwynn's Island

Just days after the Convention's adjournment, the stalemate at Gwynn's Island was shattered when General Lewis ordered two cannon batteries built along the shore to open fire upon Lord Dunmore's ships and encampment on the island. The first cannon shot reportedly blasted into the ship that Dunmore was on, nearly killing the deposed royal governor. Other shots followed from eighteen and nine pound cannon, sparking shock and panic among Dunmore's assorted fleet and in his encampment on the tip of the island. Rather than fight, Dunmore and his supporters fled. Ships were towed out of range of the guns as quickly as possible and the island was evacuated in the evening. Troops from the Seventh Virginia crossed onto Gwynn's Island the following day (July 10) and found an appalling sight. Captain Thomas Posey described it in his journal.

> *Crossed into the Island but no fighting ensued except a few shot. By one o' clock the whole of the enemy had*

---

[45] Tarter, ed., "Proceedings of the Virginia Convention, June 29 and July 1, 1776," *Revolutionary Virginia: Road to Independence*, Vol. 7, Part 2, 654-655, 668.

[46] Tarter, ed., "Proceedings of the Virginia Convention, July 5, 1776," *Revolutionary Virginia: Road to Independence*, Vol. 7, Part 2, 706.

> *evacuated and embarked...I cannot help observing, that I never saw more distress in my life, than what I found among some of the poor deluded Negroes which they could not take time, or did not chuse to carry off with them, they being sick. Those that I saw, some dying, and many calling out for help; and throughout the whole Island we found them strew'd about, many of them torn to pieces by wild beasts – great numbers of the bodies having never been buried.*[47]

Reports of Lord Dunmore's expulsion from Gwynn's Island, followed just days later by news from Philadelphia of the Declaration of Independence, created a festive atmosphere in Williamsburg. The Council of State, acting on behalf of Governor Henry, who was seriously ill at his home at Scotchtown in Hanover County, ordered Virginia's printers to publish the entire text of the Declaration and every sheriff in the commonwealth was ordered to, "*proclaim the same at the door of his courthouse the first court day after he shall have received the* [text]."[48]

The Declaration of Independence was read aloud three times in Williamsburg on July 25, "*amidst the acclamations of the people*," at the capitol, county courthouse, and governor's residence.[49] Cannon and musket salutes were fired by troops assembled for each reading.[50]

Five days earlier, the Continental Congress in Philadelphia called upon Virginia for the first time to send two of its nine continental regiments northward to reinforce General Washington and the main American army. The First and Third

---

[47] Posey, "Journal Entry, July 10, 1776," *Revolutionary War Journal*.
[48] Purdie, "July 26, 1776," and "August 2, 1776," *Virginia Gazette*, 1, 3.
[49] Purdie, "July 26, 1776," *Virginia Gazette*, 2.
[50] Ibid.

Virginia Regiments were selected and marched north in August. They were followed by the Fourth, Fifth, and Sixth regiments in September when Congress requested further reinforcements.

With the Nineth Virginia posted on the eastern shore, the Eighth Virginia in South Carolina with General Lee, and the Seventh Virginia posted in Gloucester County and Yorktown, the only continental regiment left in Williamsburg was the Second Virginia. Its time there was brief, however, because the term of enlistment for the Second Virginia's men expired in October and most refused to re-enlist under Colonel Woodford. Thus, the Second Virginia Regiment temporarily dissolved, and until new recruits were raised to re-constitute the regiment, the Seventh Virginia was the only continental regiment in the vicinity of Williamsburg.[51] General Lewis ordered the Seventh Virginia from its posts in Gloucester County and Yorktown to Williamsburg in September.[52]

The departure of Lord Dunmore and his fleet to New York and St. Augustine, Florida in August reduced the danger to Williamsburg significantly. The absence of most of Virginia's continental line from Williamsburg and the commonwealth, which amounted to several thousand troops, ushered in a degree of calm that the capital had not seen in over a year.

Nevertheless, the war continued to the north in New York and to the west with fighting against the Cherokee Indians on the frontier. The war effort in Williamsburg continued as well with the formation of six new continental regiments (authorized in mid-September by the Continental Congress). These new

---

[51] Hening, ed., "October 1776," *Statutes at Large, Being a Collection of all the Laws of Virginia…*, Vol. 9, 179.

[52] Chase and Grizzard Jr., eds., "Colonel William Crawford to General Washington, September 20, 1776," *The Papers of George Washington, Revolutionary War Series,* Vol. 6, 350-351.

troops, along with those already in the field within and beyond Virginia's borders, needed clothing, gear, and shelter.

James Anderson operated a blacksmith shop off Botetourt Street and had been the public armorer in Williamsburg since 1766, an appointment that involved maintaining Virginia's stock of weapons housed in the powder magazine and governor's palace.[53] His duties grew significantly in the summer of 1776 when his entire blacksmith shop was hired as armorers by the Committee of Safety.[54] Expansion of the site in the fall of 1776 was necessary to meet the demands of Virginia's growing armed forces.[55]

In August, several prominent Virginians, led by Robert Carter Nicholas, formed the Williamsburg Society of Manufactures to produce textiles from flax, hemp, wool and cotton.[56] They set up their manufactory at Capitol Landing on Queen's Creek, a mile and a half north of the capitol. Advertising in the newspaper for a superintendent along with spinners and weavers, the managers of the manufactory sought to purchase flax and hemp to make sail cloth and other fabric.[57] Ads placed in the gazettes in December announcing that the Manufactory was prepared to receive apprentice spinners and

---

[53] Kathrine W. Schupp, "Anderson's Blacksmith Shop: A Case for the Tinsmith among the Anvils: Block 10, Area G," Colonial Williamsburg Foundation Library Research Report Series, 406, (John D. Rockefeller Jr., Library, 2002), 9.

[54] H. R. McIlwaine, ed., "Proceedings of the Committee of Safety, July 2, 1776," *Journals of the Council of State of* Virginia, Vol. 1, (Richmond, 1931), 57.

[55] Noel Poirer, *The Williamsburg Public Armory: A Historical Study, Block 10, Building 22F*, Colonial Williamsburg Foundation Library Research Report Series, 406, (John D. Rockefeller Jr., Library, 2003), 17.

[56] Max Hamrick, *Williamsburg Manufactory: Revised and Expanded from the 1957 Report of Mills Brown*, Colonial Williamsburg Foundation Library Research Report Series, 406, (John D. Rockefeller Jr., Library, 2006), 3.

[57] Purdie, "August 23, 1776," *Virginia Gazette*, 3, and John Dixon and William Hunter, "August 24, 1776," *Virginia Gazette*, 6.

weavers and was still in need of, "*some good spinners and weavers*," suggests that production of cloth had begun before the year ended.[58] By March of the following year, a quantity of linen produced by the Manufactory was auctioned to the public in front of the Raleigh Tavern.[59]

Virginia's political leaders also acted in August to address a shortage of housing for the troops who remained in Williamsburg. Upon the recommendation of the Council of State, which called for, "*Barracks for the Continental Army stationed here to be built on that Part of the Park, which the Governor lately gave up for the use of the Troops*," Colonel William Finnie, Deputy Quarter Master General for Virginia's forces, advertised for bids in the newspaper.[60] Those interested were to build, "*a sufficient number of WOODEN BARRACKS to hold 1,000 troops, also a large STABLE for the horses belonging to the army*."[61]

The stables were necessary because the Convention had authorized the formation of six troops of light cavalry.[62] A troop of cavalry typically amounted to 35 horses and men, so stables for over 200 horses were needed if all the cavalry were to be posted in Williamsburg. Orders from Governor Henry and the Council in late September to build, "*Barracks…for one hundred Horses*," in the same location as the infantry barracks, suggests that some of the cavalry were to be posted elsewhere.[63]

---

[58] Dixon and Hunter, "December 13, 1776," *Virginia Gazette*, 1, and Purdie, "December 20, 1776," *Virginia Gazette Supplement*, 2.

[59] Dixon and Hunter, "March 21, 1777," *Virginia Gazette*, 2.

[60] McIlwaine, ed., "Proceedings of the Council of State, August 6, 1776," *Journals of the Council of State of* Virginia, Vol. 1, 109-110, and Purdie, "August 9, 1776," *Virginia Gazette*, 3.

[61] Purdie, "August 9, 1776," *Virginia Gazette*, 3.

[62] Tarter, ed., "Proceedings of the Virginia Convention, June 13, 1776," *Revolutionary Virginia: Road to Independence*, Vol. 7, Part 2, 474-477.

[63] McIlwaine, ed., "Proceedings of the Council of State, September 26, 1776," *Journals of the Council of State of* Virginia, Vol. 1, 175.

Two weeks earlier, the Council ordered General Lewis to re-consider his decision to build barracks for just a thousand men. The Council, presumably with Governor Henry's concurrence, wanted accommodations for double that number.[64]

Perhaps one reason Governor Henry and the Council insisted on larger barracks was their intention to order over a thousand militia to Williamsburg during the fall to bolster the city's defenses.[65] A committee of the House of Delegates requested within days of convening in October that the Governor and Council reconsider their order, noting that no immediate need for additional militia in Williamsburg currently existed.[66]

The Assembly's attitude changed in November when reports of British warships sailing south from New York prompted Governor Henry and the Council to summon militia to both Portsmouth and Williamsburg.[67] It is likely that at least some of the militia that arrived in Williamsburg in December, along with soldiers from the Seventh Virginia Regiment still posted in the capital, stayed in the newly built barracks in the park behind the Governor's Palace.

The Virginia General Assembly met in the capitol for the rest of the year. Archibald Cary was selected as Speaker of the Senate and Edmund Pendleton, Speaker of the House of

---

[64] McIlwaine, ed., "Proceedings of the Council of State, September 10, 1776," *Journals of the Council of State of* Virginia, Vol. 1, 153.

[65] McIlwaine, ed., "Proceedings of the Council of State, September 26, 1776," *Journals of the Council of State of* Virginia, Vol. 1, 176.

[66] Alexander Purdie, "Proceedings of the House of Delegates, October 11, 1776," *Journal of the House of Delegates of Virginia*, (Williamsburg: Alexander Purdie, 1776), 10-11.

[67] H. R. McIlwaine, ed., "Proceedings of the Council of State, November 21, 1776," and "Proceedings of the House of Delegates, Nov. 21, 1776," *Official Letters of the Governors of the State of Virginia,* Vol. 1, (Richmond: Davis Bottom, Superintendent of Public Printing, 1926), 65-66.

Delegates.[68] They and their fellow members debated such matters as how to raise six more continental regiments (per Congress's instructions) and whether to move the capital to a safer location (they did not).[69] The assembly also authorized, "*for the internal security of this country* [Virginia], *that a number of fortifications be erected at select harbors.*"[70] These posts were to be garrisoned by troops from three new state regiments, raised specifically for the defense of Virginia. Although these state garrison regiments comprised regular, full-time soldiers like the continental regiments, the garrison troops were not to serve outside of Virginia without the consent of the General Assembly.[71]

Before its legislative session ended, however, the General Assembly demonstrated how easily such a restriction could be circumvented. Shaken by reports in December that the Continental Congress had fled Philadelphia and the city's fall to the British appeared imminent, the Assembly passed an extraordinary measure on December 21, its last day in session. The legislators granted Governor Henry and the Council of State, "*additional powers...during a limited time, for the more speedy execution of the most vigorous and effectual measures to repel the invasion of the enemy.*"[72] This rather vague resolution empowered the governor and council to, "*call forth*

---

[68] Purdie, "Proceedings of the House of Delegates, October 7, 1776," *Journal of the House of Delegates of Virginia*, 3, and Purdie, "October 11, 1776," *Virginia Gazette*, 2.

[69] Purdie, "October 18, 1776," *Virginia Gazette*, 2.

[70] Hening, ed., "An Act for making a father provision for the internal security and defence of this country, October 1776," *Statutes at Large, Being a Collection of all the Laws of Virginia...*, Vol. 9, 192.

[71] Hening, ed., "An Act for making a father provision for the internal security and defence of this country, October 1776," *Statutes at Large, Being a Collection of all the Laws of Virginia...*, Vol. 9, 194.

[72] Purdie, "Proceedings of the House of Delegates, December 21, 1776," *Journal of the House of Delegates of Virginia*, 143-145.

any…military force," they deemed necessary and send them out of the commonwealth, "to join the continental army, or…[assist] *any of our sister states.*"[73] This new authority of the governor and council was to exist until the General Assembly reconvened in May, five months away.

Governor Henry and the Council wasted no time exercising their new power, proclaiming on December 26, that, "*Whereas the present critical situation of American affairs renders necessary the utmost exertion of every sister State,*" County Lieutenants (who commanded the militia of their county), were urged and required to organize companies of volunteers who were willing to, "*engage in the defence of this State, or march to the assistance of any other, should the exigency demand it.*"[74] Three days earlier, Governor Henry wrote to Cornelius Harnett, the president of the North Carolina Committee of Safety to inform him that,

> *We mean to act with vigour and upon a liberal plan. If your state will be distressed, ours will gladly contribute to its Relief if possible. Our Interests are the same, our operations shall harmonize.*[75]

Neither North Carolina or Virginia would experience significant military distress in 1777, the focus of the war remained in the mid-Atlantic region, and Virginians, both in the field and on the home front in Williamsburg, continued to do what they could to support the war effort.

---

[73] Ibid, 1.

[74] McIlwaine, ed., "A Proclamation, December 26, 1776," *Official Letters of the Governors of the State of Virginia,* Vol. 1, 86.

[75] McIlwaine, ed., "Governor Henry to Cornelius Harnett, December 23, 1776," *Official Letters of the Governors of the State of Virginia,* Vol. 1, 84.

Five

1777-1779

Virginia, unlike several other former colonies, never developed a strong Tory element within its borders. Scores of Virginians did indeed actively support Lord Dunmore while he remained in Virginia as did hundreds of runaway slaves and several thousand Virginians pledged their loyalty to the British crown in late 1775, but military setbacks at Great Bridge, Norfolk, and Gwynn's Island, smothered whatever strong loyalist support that might have developed.

Many suspected Tories and slaves who had joined, or attempted to join Dunmore and were captured by Virginia authorities, were held in the public jail within sight of the capitol. It was a horrid experience.

Built in 1702-03, the Public Gaol, as it was spelled then, was meant to hold prisoners charged with felonies while they waited for their trial, just 100 yards away in the capitol. A debtor's prison was added a few years later, built just to the west of the original prison and connected by a small walled courtyard.[1] In 1722 the prison was expanded again by the addition of a jailor's house. Debtors were kept in the east end of the complex that was formerly used by the jailer, while accused criminals were kept in the four chambers attached to the courtyard.[2] Several outbuildings were added to the complex

---

[1] Collier Harris, *Public Gaol Historical Report: Block 27, Building 2,* Colonial Williamsburg Foundation Library Research Report Series, 1628, (John D. Rockefeller Jr., Library, 1971),157-159.
[2] Ibid, 162.

in the 1740's but no other significant alteration was made to the public jail prior to the Revolutionary War.[3]

The first prisoners held at the jail as a result of the Revolutionary War were slaves who attempted to flee to Lord Dunmore in 1775. Hundreds did so successfully in response to Dunmore's offer in November of freedom to any male slave of a rebel who fought for the royal governor and crown. Scores of slaves fled to Dunmore even before his offer and some were caught and held in the public jail in Williamsburg.[4]

The number of prisoners held at the jail increased significantly after the battle of Great Bridge in early December 1775. Seventeen Tory and eleven black prisoners, all captured at Great Bridge, were lodged in the jail at the start of 1776.[5] Josias Rogers, an imprisoned British sailor captured on the Eastern Shore, was brought to the jail in May of 1776. His memoirs, written in the third person, describe the conditions he encountered.

> *At Williamsburgh his confinement was more horrid than it had ever been; he was thrown into a vile jail, among criminals of all denominations. The vault* [holding human waste] *was full and began to overflow; the weather became intolerably hot, the airhole was small...they were covered with vermin; and* [the] *itch broke out among them, and the jail-fever* [typhus] *began to appear.*[6]

---

[3] Ibid, 171.

[4] John Pinkney, "November 30, 1775," *Virginia Gazette*, 3.

[5] Purdie, "January 5, 1776," *Virginia Gazette Supplement*, 2.

[6] William Gilpin, ed., *Memoirs of Josias Rogers, Esq., Commander of His Majesty's Ship Quebec*, (London: T. Cadell and W. Davies Strand, 1808), 20.

A committee appointed by the Fifth Virginia Convention to investigate the conditions of the jail confirmed much of Rogers's account, blaming it on the poor design of the jail.

> *It appeared to* [the committee] *that the said Gaol being badly planned and situated for the purpose of admitting a free Air all the Prisoners are more or less distressed on that Account* [and] *this Inconvenience is greatly increased...by a large number of Persons being under Confinement in the same small apartment as the heat of the Weather that although most of the rooms seem to have been properly attended to and kept in tolerable decency an offensive smell which they think would be injurious to the most robust health prevails in them all but which they think might in a great measure be removed by burning Tar in and frequently purifying the rooms with Vinegar. That the room in which the Negroes are confined abounds with filth, a Circumstance as they are informed owing to the want of necessary hands to assist in providing for so large and unusual number of Prisoners....*[7]

The Convention ordered the recommended changes and sent Josias Rogers, who was a prisoner of war, to Charlottesville, where he was granted his parole on the promise that he would not depart the town.[8]

Despite efforts to address the abysmal conditions, the number of suspected spies, counterfeiters, Tories, deserters, as well as runaway slaves and criminals, overwhelmed the public

---

[7] Tarter, ed., "Proceedings of the Fifth Virginia Convention, June 7, 1776," *Revolutionary Virginia: Road to Independence*, Vol. 7, Part 1, 389.
[8] Ibid, 390.

jail in 1777.[9] Several escapes occurred in the spring that prompted an investigation of the jailor, Peter Pelham. A legislative committee concluded that Pelham's, "*want of care*" was responsible for the successful escapes and called for his dismissal, but the entire legislature disagreed and he remained at his post.[10] Within a year, however, the assembly granted the governor and Council of State authority to superintend and regulate the public jail.[11]

The governor and Council of State also exercised their authority to renew their arrangement with James Anderson for blacksmith work done for the commonwealth. They agreed to rent his shop and services for all of 1777.[12] An additional forge was built at public expense on Anderson's property in late 1776 and the council made arrangements to rent both forges as well as six sets of tools and eight vices for the "*Gunsmith's Business*."[13] Stipends were also provided to pay the wages and board of Anderson's workmen and he was authorized to, "*employ such other workmen as the public Business requires on the best terms he can, and charge the country with whatever wages he pays.*"[14]

---

[9] Harris, *Public Gaol Historical Report: Block 27, Building 2*, Colonial Williamsburg Foundation Library Research Report Series, 406, 190.
[10] Helen Bullock, *Public Gaol Historical Report: Block 27, Building 2, Lot 1*, Colonial Williamsburg Foundation Library Research Report Series 1511, (John D. Rockefeller Jr., Library, 1930-34), 137-138.
[11] Hening, ed., "An act to empower the Governour and Council to superintend and regulate the Public Jail. May 1778," *Statutes at Large, Being a Collection of all the Laws of Virginia…*, Vol. 9, 478-479.
[12] McIlwaine, ed., "Proceedings of the Council of State, March 21, 1777," *Journals of the Council of State of* Virginia, Vol. 1, 373.
[13] Poirer, *The Williamsburg Public Armory: A Historical Study, Block 10, Building 22F*, Colonial Williamsburg Foundation Library Research Report Series, 406, 16-17, and McIlwaine, ed., "Proceedings of the Council of State, March 21, 1777," *Journals of the Council of State of* Virginia, Vol. 1, 373.
[14] McIlwaine, ed., "Proceedings of the Council of State, March 21, 1777," *Journals of the Council of State of* Virginia, Vol. 1, 373.

By the end of 1777, nine smiths were busy on Anderson's property, which was now referred to as the public armory.[15] Expansion continued in 1778 with the construction of three more forge chimneys, bringing to five in operation.[16] Archeological digs on the property suggest that the blacksmiths and gunsmiths were not the only ones employed in Anderson's public armory. Evidence of tinsmiths, gun stockers, nailers, farriers, button makers and file cutters were found by archeologists.[17] By 1779, Anderson's workforce consisted of between 40-50 workers drawn from American and French soldiers, enslaved and free blacks, convict labor, indentured servants, and several Scottish Highland prisoners of war.[18]

The Williamsburg Society of Manufactures, located on Queen's Creek at Capitol Landing, expanded its operations in 1777 as well. In May, the Society announced in the gazettes that,

> *We purpose to purchase rough Materials for manufacturing, and when wrought up to vend the same. To the Planter and Farmer we leave the Business of raising Hemp, Flax, Cotton, and Wool; and for any of these Articles, we give ready Money.*

---

[15] Poirer, *The Williamsburg Public Armory: A Historical Study, Block 10, Building 22F*, Colonial Williamsburg Foundation Library Research Report Series, 406, 18.

[16] Ibid, 19-20.

[17] Schupp, *Anderson's Blacksmith Shop: A Case for the Tinsmith Among the Anvils, Block 10, Area G*, Colonial Williamsburg Foundation Library Research Report Series 1690, 11, and Robert Foss, *James Anderson Archeological Report, Block 10, Building 22, Lot 18*, Colonial Williamsburg Foundation Library Research Report Series 1227, (John D. Rockefeller Jr., Library, 1977), 83, and Dixon and Nicolson, "June 19, 1779," *Virginia Gazette*, 3.

[18] Schupp, *Anderson's Blacksmith Shop: A Case for the Tinsmith Among the Anvils, Block 10, Area G*, Colonial Williamsburg Foundation Library Research Report Series 1690, 11.

> *We sell Hemp and Flax in small Quantities, properly prepared for spinning.*[19]

The Society added that encouragement would be given to spinners and that they were in immediate need of a mistress spinner and a wool comber, as long as they were well recommended.[20] In August, the Society announced a further expansion of its operations in order to process more hemp.

> *For want of a HEMP MILL, we have not been able to answer the continual demands on us for dressed hemp; but we have a mill now erecting and hope shortly to be able to accommodate our customers. We give ready money for cotton, wool, flax and hemp, and continue to dress the last two of those articles for others in the best and most expeditious manner. Our price for heckling is one sixth part of the gross flax or hemp.*[21]

A month before this announcement, the Society offered at public auction in front of the Raleigh Tavern, 400 yards of hemp linen fabric as well as a large piece of fine linen fabric woven at the manufactory.[22]

Quarterly meetings of the Society's investors were held at the Raleigh tavern through 1780 and the manufactory apparently continued operations until 1784, but little is known of its output after 1777.[23]

---

[19] John Dixon, "May 16, 1777," *Virginia Gazette*, 2.
[20] Ibid.
[21] Purdie, "August 15, 1777," *Virginia Gazette*, 2.
[22] Purdie, "July 25, 1777," *Virginia Gazette*, 2.
[23] Hamrick, *Williamsburg Manufactory: Revised and Expanded from the 1957 Report of Mills Brown*, Colonial Williamsburg Foundation Library Research Report Series, 406, 5.

With the General Assembly not scheduled to re-convene until May of 1777, Governor Patrick Henry, (who took up residence in the Governor's Palace in the summer of 1776), and the Council of State jointly governed Virginia. In late May, Henry hosted a large delegation of Cherokee leaders who had come to Williamsburg to ratify a peace treaty.[24] Dixon and Hunter's *Virginia Gazette* reported that,

> *Upwards of forty gentlemen and ladies of the Cherokee nation are now on a negotiation of peace.... They have had an audience, and it is expected a compact will be settled with them in a few days. Among them are Oconostota, the Little Carpenter, the Pigeon, and other headmen and warriors. After the Talk was concluded, they favoured the public with a dance on the green in front of the palace, where a considerable number of spectators, both male and female, were agreeably entertained.*[25]

The Virginia General Assembly, which convened in the capitol that same month, focused most, but not all, of its effort on war measures. In early June, however, a social affair of music and dancing was held at the Capitol.[26] Ebenezer Hazard, a visitor from New York, described the affair.

> *The Entertainment last Night was very fine, the Music excellent, the Assembly large & polite, & the Ladies*

---

[24] McIlwaine, ed., "Gov. Henry to Geo. Wythe, Speaker of the House of Delegates, May 27, 1777," *Official Letters of the Governors of the State of Virginia,* Vol. 1, 154.
[25] Dixon and Hunter, "May 30, 1777," *Virginia Gazette*, 2.
[26] Jane Carson, ed., "Diary Entry of Ebenezer Hazard, June 5, 1777," *We Were There: Descriptions of Williamsburg, 1699-1859*, (Charlottesville: The University Press of Virginia, 1965), 38.

> *made a brilliant Appearance. A Mr. Blagrave (a Clergyman), his Lady, & a Mrs. Neal, performed the vocal Parts; they sang well, especially Mr. Blagrave. His Lady played excellently on the Harpsichord. After the Entertainment was over, the Company went upstairs to dance.*[27]

Mr. Hazard included other observations of Williamsburg made during his visit in the summer and again in the winter of 1777. They provide some insight about life in the city in 1777. Hazard noted in June that,

> *The Virginians, even in the city, do not pay proper Attention to Decency in the Appearance of their Negroes; I have seen Boys of 10 & 12 Years of Age going through the Streets quite naked, & others with only Part of a Shirt hanging Part of the Way down their Backs. This is so common a Sight that even the Ladies do not appear to be shocked at it.*[28]

On his second trip to Williamsburg in December 1777, Mr. Hazard observed that,

> *There is a severe Act of Assembly against Gaming, but I observe the Members of that House are as much addicted to it as other Men, & as frequently transgress the Law. I have known one of them bet 30 Dollars*

---

[27] Ibid.

[28] Carson, ed., "Diary Entry of Ebenezer Hazard, June 8, 1777," *We Were There: Descriptions of Williamsburg, 1699-1859*, 39.

> *upon an odd Trick at Whist. Gaming is amazingly prevalent in Wmsburg.*[29]

When the General Assembly was not engaged in gaming or dancing, it conducted business in the capitol, and in in the summer of 1777, that business focused on passing laws to better regulate the militia, recruit troops for both continental and state regiments, and manage Virginia's war finances.[30] The Assembly agreed to send one of Virginia's three state garrison regiments, raised specifically for the defense of the commonwealth, northward to reinforce General Washington. They also extended the additional powers it had granted the governor and council of state during its last adjournment to the next general assembly session in October.[31]

Although there had been little need to exercise these additional powers in the first half of 1777, Governor Henry and the Council did call out militia from the surrounding counties in February upon reports of British warships in Chesapeake Bay. Fifty men from the counties of James City, New Kent, Hanover, and King William were ordered to Williamsburg to guard the magazines located in the capital. Other counties sent men to Yorktown and Hampton to protect those vulnerable coastal towns.[32]

---

[29] Carson, ed., "Diary Entry of Ebenezer Hazard, December 13, 1777," *We Were There: Descriptions of Williamsburg, 1699-1859*, 42.

[30] Hening, ed., "Proceedings of the Virginia General Assembly, May 1777," *The Statutes at Large; Being a Collection of all the Laws of Virginia….*, Vol. 9, 267-305.

[31] McIlwaine, ed., "Proceedings of the Council of State, June 14, 1777," *Journals of the Council of State of* Virginia, Vol. 1, 432, and Hening, ed., "Proceedings of the Virginia General Assembly, May 1777," *The Statutes at Large; Being a Collection of all the Laws of Virginia….*, Vol. 9, 309.

[32] McIlwaine, ed., "Journal of the Council, February 5, 1777," *Official Letters of the Governors of the State of Virginia,* Vol. 1, 98.

Nothing came of the British presence in February nor again in August when an enormous British fleet sailed into Chesapeake Bay. It was General William Howe's army, making its way up the bay to attack Philadelphia. Governor Henry was at his home at Scotchtown when the news arrived, so Virginia's response was left to Lieutenant Governor John Page and the Council. Concerned that Virginia was the enemy's target, Page and the Council called for militia from nearly twenty counties as far west as Bedford County and as far north as Spotsylvania County to rush troops to Williamsburg to defend the capital.[33] They were to be joined by the three battalions of state regulars raised earlier in the year for the defense of the commonwealth.[34] Within a week of this appeal, approximately 600 militia, including a company comprised of faculty and students from the college of William and Mary, were in Williamsburg, and many more troops were expected.[35] By the end of the month, approximately 4,000 troops were posted in Williamsburg, Yorktown, and Hampton to guard against an expected British attack.[36]

This proved unnecessary, for General Howe's attention was focused on Philadelphia, not Virginia, and most of the militia were dismissed from further duty.[37] This was likely a relief to many residents of Williamsburg who found the constant challenges of sentries posted about town annoying. This issue was addressed by the Council of State on September 16.

---

[33] McIlwaine, ed., "Proceedings of the Council of State, August 16, 1777," *Journals of the Council of State of* Virginia, Vol. 1, 467.
[34] McIlwaine, ed., "Proceedings of the Council of State, August 21, 1777," *Journals of the Council of State of* Virginia, Vol. 1, 471.
[35] Dixon and Hunter, "August 22, 1777," *Virginia Gazette*, 2.
[36] Selby, *The Revolution in Virginia: 1775-1783*, 134.
[37] McIlwaine, ed., "Proceedings of the Council of State, September 13-17, 1777," *Journals of the Council of State of* Virginia, Vol. 1, 488-491.

> *It being represented to the Lieutenant Governor that the Inhabitants of the City of Williamsburg labour under great Inconvenience from the Instructions at present given to the Soldiers upon Guard in Consequence of which they often Interrupt innocent people from pursuing their Business, however urgent, which appears to be a useless Severity, and a great Infringement of the Rights of the People,* [the Council recommended] *to the Commanding officer of the Troops at this Station, to give strict Charge to the several Centinels posted in the City not to challenge or Stop any person whatever while passing quietly in any of the Streets....*[38]

The Council also called for street patrols from 10 p.m. to reveille to detain any disorderly persons as well as any, "*Negro, or other Servant*," unless he or she be on an errand for their Master or Mistress.[39]

Reports from the north of General Washington's defeat at Brandywine, followed by reports of the fall of Philadelphia to General Howe, dampened Virginia's spirits. The 2nd Virginia State Regiment, along with hundreds of militia from the northern counties of Virginia, were sent north to reinforce Washington, but the American cause looked bleak.[40]

News of a stunning American victory over General John Burgoyne in Saratoga, New York lifted the gloomy mood in

---

[38] McIlwaine, ed., "Proceedings of the Council of State, September 16, 1777," *Journals of the Council of State of* Virginia, Vol. 1, 490.
[39] Ibid.
[40] McIlwaine, ed., "Proceedings of the Council of State, August 30 – September 1, 1777," *Journals of the Council of State of* Virginia, Vol. 1, 478 479.

Williamsburg in late October. Purdie's *Virginia Gazette* reported on October 31 that,

> *Upon receiving this great and glorious news a general joy diffused itself amongst all ranks, the regular troops and militia of the city were instantly paraded, and both from artillery and small arms resounded the glad tidings. The inhabitants illuminated their houses, and with the gentlemen of the General Assembly, spent a cheerful and agreeable evening, wherein the names of WASHINGTON, GATES, ARNOLD, LINCOLN, etc. etc. were often bumpered with huzzas to the independence of America.*[41]

The Continental Congress called for a day of thanksgiving to be observed on November 13, and Governor Henry proclaimed it so in Virginia. A somber observation of the momentous victory at Saratoga took place that day. Purdie's gazette reported that, "*in the forenoon, to a very crowded audience, the Reverend Mr. Bracken delivered an excellent discourse on the glad occasion; and* [in the] *afternoon...the Reverend Mr. Madison, chaplain and President of the College, preached an animating sermon.*"[42]

The following evening, reported Purdie, a celebration of the victory at Saratoga erupted again.

> *The Members of the General Assembly gave a grand ball and entertainment at the Capitol, at which were present all the ladies and gentlemen in this city and its neighborhood, many from different parts of the*

---

[41] Purdie, "October 31, 1777," *Virginia Gazette*, 2.

[42] Dixon and Hunter, "October 31, 1777," *Virginia Gazette*, 2, and Purdie, "November 21, 1777," *Virginia Gazette*, 2.

> *country, the military gentlemen, and the strangers then in town. Thirteen rounds from two pieces of cannon placed before the Capitol, the names of Washington, Gates, etc., etc., announcing each discharge, preceded the festivities, during which gaiety and good humour enlivened the ball, and socialness and jollity presided at the banquet.*[43]

In the weeks following Philadelphia's fall to the British it was hoped that American defenses and obstacles in the Delaware River would prevent a sufficient supply of food and other necessaries from reaching the British army in the city. If the Americans could deny the British navy access to Philadelphia long enough, General Howe and his troops might be forced to abandon the city and return to New York.

Alas, in mid-November Fort Mifflin, one of the key American forts defending the river obstructions, fell to the British. By December, a British naval supply line to Philadelphia was secure enough to allow them to comfortably remain in the city over the winter. General Washington established a winter camp for his army about 25 miles to the northwest of Philadelphia, at Valley Forge.

1778

The General Assembly, which re-convened in the capitol in late October, completed its business in late January 1778. Edmund Pendleton, who missed the first few weeks of the assembly due to a leg injury, served as Speaker of the House of Delegates. He summed up his experience with the legislature to his friend, General William Woodford, who was with Washington's army at Valley Forge.

---

[43] Purdie, "November 21, 1777," *Virginia Gazette*, 2.

I have at length reached home after an Absence of near 10 weeks and pretty hard service in the Assembly, which Adjourned...after a tedious Session, greatly protracted by the difficulty and Novelty of drafting men to recruit the Army, and the mode of taxation.[44]

The departure of the assembly once again left Governor Henry (who was re-elected to a second term as governor in late May of 1777 and the Council of State, to govern Virginia. Governor Henry, however, returned to Scotchtown for a few weeks upon the adjournment of the assembly and did not return to Williamsburg until late February. In his absence the council, under Lieutenant Governor John Page, carried on, mostly issuing warrants for payment of war expenses. Governor Henry returned to Williamsburg on February 19, and resumed his leadership of the council and government.[45]

The struggle to raise troops to replace those in Virginia's first nine continental regiments whose enlistments expired in the spring of 1778 continued with limited success. In mid-April, Governor Henry sent a circular letter to all the County Lieutenants in Virginia urging them to prepare their militia for service.

The design of this address is to require your most strenuous exertions to get your militia in readiness. In a particular manner, I entreat your attention to the arms and accoutrements of the men, and to see that

---

[44] Mays, ed., "Edmund Pendleton to General William Woodford, January 31, 1778," *The Letters and Papers of Edmund Pendleton*, Vol. 1, 246.
[45] H. R. McIlwaine, ed., "Proceedings of the Council of State, February 19, 1778," *Journals of the Council of State of Virginia*, Vol. 2, (Richmond: 1932), 86.

one third part of them be put into readiness to march at a moment's warning.[46]

A week earlier, the council informed Governor Henry that militia ordered from the counties of New Kent and Surry to help guard the capital were insufficient and recommended that he call militia from Charles City County to Williamsburg as well.[47] There was no immediate threat to Virginia to trigger these actions, just an expectation that with warmer weather would come increased military activity from the enemy.

Some of this anxiety was relieved in mid-May by news of an American alliance with France.[48] Aside from the proceedings of the General Assembly (which reconvened in May and June) and Council of State, the documentary record for late May and early June in Williamsburg is sporadic, so it is difficult to determine the reaction of Williamsburg's inhabitants to the news, but one can imagine it was well received and sparked many toasts in honor of France.

At the end of May, Governor Henry was re-elected to a third term as governor of Virginia by the General Assembly, which concluded its business in early June. Thomas Jefferson attended the assembly and reported to his friend Richard Henry Lee, who was a delegate to the Continental Congress in York, Pennsylvania, that their decision to authorize a regiment of cavalry was the only act he believed would help the American army. Jefferson viewed the legislature's continued reliance on volunteers to supplement its continental soldiers as foolhardy

---

[46] McIlwaine, ed., "Gov. Henry's Circular Letter, April 12, 1778," *Official Letters of the Governors of the State of Virginia,* Vol. 1, 265.

[47] McIlwaine, ed., "Proceedings of the Council of State, April 4, 1778," *Journals of the Council of State of Virginia,* Vol. 2, 115.

[48] Dixon and Hunter, "May 15, 1778," *Virginia Gazette*, 3.

and doomed to fail.[49] He closed his letter with news of the arrival of a large French ship with, "*a vast cargo of woollens...stockings, shoes, etc. fit for the army [and] fifty thousand weight of powder....*"[50]

As some of the items in the shipment were better suited for private use rather than military use, the Council of State arranged with Robert Prentis to rent four of his storehouses located on Duke of Gloucester Street. He was to, "*take charge & dispose of such Articles as are to be sold to the Inhabitants at large*," and was paid 35 pounds a month for his trouble and 15 pounds a month for the use of his buildings.[51]

In mid-June, Governor Henry confirmed Thomas Jefferson's fears about the inability of Virginia to raise its quota of troops for continental service, informing Congress that,

> *The Assembly at their late Sitting, have directed three hundred and fifty Cavalry, & two thousand Infantry to be forthwith raised, & to join the grand Army. Some of the former will be raised, but from every appearance, I am sorry to say, there is but too little reason to expect any success in getting the Infantry.*[52]

Virginia's struggle to recruit more troops continued for the rest of the war, but it had little impact on events in 1778. The new treaty between America and France strategically altered

---

[49] Julian P. Boyd, ed., "Thomas Jefferson to Richard Henry Lee, June 5, 1778," *The Papers of Thomas Jefferson*, Vol. 2, (Princeton, NJ: Princeton University Press, 1950), 194.
[50] Ibid.
[51] McIlwaine, ed., "Proceedings of the Council of State, June 12, and June 22, 1778," *Journals of the Council of State of Virginia,* Vol. 2, 149, 152.
[52] McIlwaine, ed., "Gov, Henry to the President of Congress, Henry Laurens, June 18, 1778," *Official Letters of the Governors of the State of Virginia,* Vol. 1, 289-290.

the conflict for Great Britain, so much so that it caused General Henry Clinton, the new British commander in America, to abandon Philadelphia in June and return to New York. Unable to move his entire force by ship, Clinton marched the bulk of his British army across New Jersey, pursued by General Washington, who caught the British near Monmouth Courthouse. The day long clash that ensued ended in a draw, but the British retreat to Sandy Hook under cover of darkness made the Battle of Monmouth feel like an American victory.

The war in the north entered a new phase with General Clinton's return to New York. Both main armies were largely stationary for the remainder of the year. Conflict on the Virginia frontier drew the attention of Virginia's leaders as did a British expedition to the south late in the year, but Williamsburg still seemed far from the war and carried on as usual with bi-annual meetings of the General Assembly, regular legal proceedings in both the district and county courts, and the general commerce of war.

Apart from preparations for the arrival of British and Hessian prisoners captured at Saratoga in 1777 (they were to be placed under guard in Charlottesville) and promising news of success against the Indians far to the west by Colonel George Rogers Clark, the situation in Williamsburg remained unchanged for the remainder of 1778.

One important bill passed by the General Assembly in its fall session that deserves notice was a prohibition on the further importation of slaves into Virginia from overseas or another state. The new law specified that, "*Every slave imported into this commonwealth, contrary to the true intent and meaning of this act, shall upon such importation become free.*"[53]

---

[53] Hening, ed., "An Act for Preventing the farter Importation of Slaves, October, 1778," *Statutes at Large*, Vol. 9, 471.

Exceptions were granted to slave owners from other states who settled in Virginia with their slaves and Virginians who owned slaves in other states and chose to bring them to Virginia.[54]

1779

By the spring of 1779, encouraging reports in the newspapers about new European support for America gave Virginians hope that the long conflict with Britain was drawing to a victorious conclusion.[55] Such good news, coupled with a sense of war fatigue and wishful thinking, generated a degree of military complacency that left the commonwealth vulnerable to attack. This vulnerability was exposed in early May when a British naval force sailed into Chesapeake Bay.

Mathew-Collier Raid

The British flotilla, which included 6 powerful warships, several privateers, and 22 transport ships carrying 1,800 British and German troops, arrived off Virginia on May 8.[56] This combined land and naval force, commanded by General Edward Mathew and Commodore Sir George Collier, was sent from New York by General Clinton to disrupt the flow of Virginia reinforcements to both General Washington in New York and General Benjamin Lincoln in South Carolina. Six months earlier, General Clinton had sent another British force to Georgia which easily captured Savannah and created a new front in the war. This current raid on Virginia was designed in part to distract the commonwealth from sending reinforcements

---

[54] Ibid, 472.
[55] Dixon and Nicolson, "February 26 and March 19, 1779," *Virginia Gazette*, 3.
[56] Davies, ed., "Sir George Collier to Lord George Germain, May 22, 1779," *Documents of the American Revolution: 1770-83*, Vol. 17, 131.

to the south or the north. It achieved success with the latter goal, but not the former.

Most of the British fleet entered Hampton Roads on May 9, and continued into the Elizabeth River. The largest warship, H.M.S. *Raisonable* (64 guns), anchored off Hampton while H.M.S. *Otter* (14 guns) and several privateers sailed up Chesapeake Bay to harass whatever shipping they encountered.[57] The British easily captured a fort protecting Portsmouth and landed the bulk of their troops there. A detachment marched southwestward to Suffolk and burned a large supply of provisions and naval stores as well as most of the town.[58]

The General Assembly was in session when word of the British expedition reached Williamsburg but it was Governor Henry who took charge, issuing a proclamation on May 14 that required,

> *The county Lieutenants and other military officers in this commonwealth, and especially those on navigable waters, to hold their respective militias in readiness to oppose attempts of the enemy wheresoever they may be made.*[59]

Virginians responded to Henry's appeal and within days, the capital saw hundreds of militia in its streets. Major Robert Forsyth, a supernumerary continental officer in Williamsburg, observed that,

---

[57] Ibid, and Charles Stedman, *The History of the Origin, Progress, and Termination of the American War*, Vol. 2, (London: 1794), 137.
[58] "Major General Mathew to General Sir Henry Clinton, May 16, 1779," *William and Mary Quarterly, Second Series*, Vol. 12, No. 3, July 1932, 185.
[59] McIlwaine, ed., "Proclamation of Governor Patrick Henry, May 15, 1779," *Official Letters of the Governors of the State of Virginia,* Vol. 1, 370.

> *Volunteer companys turn out from all quarters, and all hands appear to be full of fight...We have about six hundred Troops, mostly militia in* [Williamsburg] *and about that number at Hampton....*[60]

Although the militia appeared willing to fight, Major Forsyth feared they would not be able to do so. "*Never was a State in such a confused helpless situation – no Arms nor accoutrements.... The Arms in the hands of our Militia are very few and in general bad.*"[61]

Virginia's militia were not the only troops tapped to repulse the British invasion. Brigadier-General Charles Scott of the continental army was in Williamsburg in 1779 and acted to assist his native state. General Scott was a veteran of Trenton, Princeton, Brandywine, Germantown, and Monmouth. He returned to Virginia on furlough the previous winter and assisted in the recruitment of new troops for the American army. Granted special authority by the General Assembly and Governor Henry to, "*do as he pleases and order matters as he thinks proper*," General Scott ordered the Virginia continental recruits, some 800 strong, who were about to march to New York to instead march to Williamsburg to protect the capital.[62]

Once again Williamsburg turned into an armed camp, but the effort proved unnecessary. The British expedition was only a raid to disrupt Virginia, not occupy it, and by late May, the British sailed away, having inflicted an estimated two million

---

[60] Showman, ed., "Major Robert Forsyth to General Greene, May 19, 1779," *The Papers of General Nathanael Greene*, Vol. 4, 48.
[61] Ibid.
[62] Edward G. Lengel, ed., "General Scott to General Washington, May 12, 1779," *The Papers of George Washington*, Vol. 20, (Charlottesville: University of Virginia Press, 2010), 457.

pounds of losses to Virginians in damaged and stolen property.[63]

Governor Henry's third term of office expired at the end of the month and he was constitutionally prohibited from serving another term. One of his last acts as governor was to host an impromptu visit of several continental and state garrison officers at the Governor's Palace on May 30. Lieutenant Baylor Hill of the First Light Dragoons recorded the affair in his diary.

> *This morning I breakfasted with Col. Porterfield at the Barracks and after; we went to town and at nine o' clock I went in company of several to a Tavern near the College to drink punch where we were join*[ed] *by others on the same business and by Eleven o' Clock the whole Company was very happy. And at breaking up the society, we concluded to pay the Governor a visit; upon wch Capt D...was to go first and inform him of our intentions. Col. Porterfield being the oldest officer present, he took the Command, and march*[ed us] *in the best for his detachment amounting in the whole to eleven, into the Pallace, where we were reciev'd by his Excelency in Person, we staid and see the last of a very large bowl of Grogg, and then we beet a march to the barracks In and about William's burg....*[64]

The General Assembly chose Thomas Jefferson as the commonwealth's next governor two days later. Dealing with

---

[63] Selby, *The Revolution in Virginia, 1775-1783,* 208.
[64] John T. Hayes, ed., *A Gentleman of Fortune, The Diary of Baylor Hill, First Continental Light Dragoons, 1777-1781*, Vol. 2, (Saddlebagg Press, 1995), 56-58.

the aftermath of the British raid fell to Jefferson, his Council of State, and the Virginia Assembly.

Six

The Capital No Longer 1779 - 1781

Three days before Jefferson was elected governor by the General Assembly, a committee from the House of Delegates, which included Jefferson as a member, introduced a bill to move the capital from Williamsburg to Richmond.[1] Jefferson had proposed a similar measure three years earlier in response to the growing influence of the burgesses from the western counties who desired a more centralized capital. The proposal was easily defeated then, but three years later, armed with the additional argument of the vulnerability of Williamsburg to British attack, a vulnerability demonstrated just days earlier with the Mathew-Collier expedition, proponents of a move narrowly won the day.

Richmond was just a small town situated at the fall line of the James River and in no way prepared to serve as Virginia's capital in 1779, so the bill authorized the construction of temporary buildings, "*for the sitting of the general assembly, courts of justice, and the several boards* [War and Trade]…."[2] The process would take time and not be completed until the following year. For the rest of 1779, Virginia's government remained in Williamsburg. This delay in implementing the General Assembly's decision might account for the lack of

---

[1] Boyd, ed., "Bill for the Removal of the Seat of Government of Virginia, May 29, 1779," *The Papers of Thomas Jefferson*, Vol. 2, 272.

[2] Hening, ed., "An Act for the Removal of the Seat of Government, May 1779," *Statutes at Large being a Collection of all the Laws of Virginia….*, (Richmond: George Cochran, 1822), Vol. 10, 88.

notice of the legislature's action in the weekly gazettes. The attention of the inhabitants of Williamsburg seemed inexplicably focused on other issues in the summer of 1779.

Henry "Hair Buyer Hamilton

The arrival of Lieutenant Governor Henry "Hair Buyer" Hamilton, the captured British governor of Detroit, caused a sensation in the capital in mid-June.[3] Charged with, "*inciting the Indians to perpetrate their accustomed cruelties on the citizens of these states, without distinction of age, sex, or condition*...[and with] *cruel and inhumane treatment*," of both Virginia's civilians and soldiers, Governor Jefferson and the Council of State ordered that Hamilton and two other prisoners with him, "*be put in irons, confined in the dungeon of the publick jail,* [denied] *the use of pen, ink, and paper, and excluded all converse except with their keeper*."[4]

Such harsh treatment was rare, particularly for someone of Hamilton's social status, but his reputation for paying Indians for the scalps of settlers along with reports of cruel treatment of prisoners sealed his fate in Williamsburg. Hamilton described his arrival and first day imprisoned in the jail in a journal that ended on June 16, 1779.

> *By the time we reached the Palace (as it is called) the Governor's residence, our escort of curious persons had become very numerous.... At the jail we were received by the jailor.... We had for our domicile a place not ten feet square by actual measurement, the only light admitted was thro' the grating of the door which opened into the Court...the light and air are*

---

[3] Dixon and Nicolson, "June 19, 1779," *Virginia Gazette*, 3.

[4] Boyd, ed., "Order of Virginia Council Placing Henry Hamilton and Others in Irons, June 16, 1779," *The Papers of Thomas Jefferson*, Vol. 2, 292-294.

> *nearly excluded, for the bars of this grating were from three to four inches thick. In one corner of this snug mansion was fixed a kind of Throne which had been of use to such miscreants as us for 60 years past, and in certain points of wind rendered the air truly* [intolerable]. *Opposite the door and nearly adjoining the throne was a little Skuttle 5 or 6 inches wide, thro which our Victual was thrust to us.*[5]

Shackled in leg irons for nearly two months and denied the comforts and liberties normally afforded a captured officer, Hamilton's treatment became a significant issue for the Virginia government, who was accused by the British of mistreating him.[6] Disagreement over the conditions of his parole kept him a captive until October of the following year when he was finally paroled and in 1781, officially exchanged.[7]

Rampant Inflation

In July, the inhabitants of Williamsburg gathered (likely at the county courthouse) to address a pressing concern throughout America, rampant price inflation (caused by the depreciation of paper money (which was printed to excess) and chronic supply shortages caused by the four year war with Britain. A committee was formed from those in attendance and it recommended that strict price controls based on a formula of 50 pounds of Virginia paper currency to one pound of sterling, be implemented in the city. The inhabitants agreed and then

---

[5] John D. Barhart, ed., *Henry Hamilton and George Rogers Clark in the American Revolution with the Unpublished Journals of Lieut. Gov. Henry Hamilton*, (Crawfordsville, IN: R. E. Banta, 1951), 204-205.

[6] Julian P. Boyd, ed., "Thomas Jefferson to George Washington, October 1, 1779," *The Papers of Thomas Jefferson*, Vol. 3, (Princeton, NJ: Princeton University Press, 1951), 97.

[7] Selby, *The Revolution in Virginia*, 197.

formed a fifteen person committee of inspection to enforce the measure.[8] The Williamsburg Committee of Inspection of 1779 included:

Samuel Beall	James Innes	James Southall
Humphrey Harwood	Henry Tazwell	Samuel Griffin
Robert Anderson	John Minson Galt	Benjamin Powell
Champion Travers	Robert Anderson	John Dixon
Edward Archer	James McClurg	John Boush[9]

Those in attendance of the meeting threatened vague consequences to anyone who violated the price controls and promised to hold violators up, "*to the publick as inimical to the rights and liberties of America.*"[10] Anticipating that these new measures might spark an exodus of goods from the city, the inhabitants agreed to require a permit from the committee to remove goods from Williamsburg valued in excess of 500 pounds. Those caught doing so without a permit risked confiscation of their goods.[11]

York County adopted similar resolves at the end of July and Warwick and Elizabeth City County followed suit in August.[12] In its last legislative session in Williamsburg in the fall of 1779, the General Assembly passed measures to raise more revenue through taxes, but did little to address the

[8] Dixon and Nicolson, "July 24 1779," *Virginia Gazette*, 1-2.
[9] Ibid, 2.
[10] Ibid.
[11] Ibid.
[12] Dixon and Nicolson, "July 31 and August 14, 1779," *Virginia Gazette*, 3

depreciation of its currency and runaway inflation.[13] The assembly adjourned on December 24, 1779, after it ordered the clerk to send all the assembly's books, papers, and records to Richmond.[14]

Moving the Capital: 1780

Relocating the capital to Richmond took months and did not begin in earnest until the start of 1780. The inhabitants of Williamsburg undoubtedly hoped the General Assembly would reverse its decision, but that did not happen. The city had always been economically dependent on commerce generated as the seat of government for Virginia, and the loss of this commerce prompted many residents to move with the government to Richmond.

Edmund Randolph advertised in the newspaper in late January 1780 that he intended to move to the new capital to continue his law practice and Benjamin Powell, a prominent building contractor, advertised his home in Williamsburg for sale in early February.[15] Another contractor, Philip Moody, was appointed by the Board of War to oversee construction of several public buildings in Richmond and James Anderson was appointed to manage a new public armory to be built in Richmond.[16] After nearly three years of expansion, the armory in Williamsburg was to be relocated to the new capital. Taverns

---

[13] Hening, ed., "An Act for Raising a Supply of Money for the Service of the United States, October 1779," *Statutes at Large*, Vol. 10, 165-171.

[14] Arthur P. Middleton and Edward M. Riley, *The Capitol: A Manual of Interpretation Designed Principally for the Use of the Hostesses and Escorts of Colonial Williamsburg*, Colonial Williamsburg Foundation Library Research Report Series, 205, 10.

[15] Dixon and Nicolson, "January 22, and February 5, 1780," *Virginia Gazette*, 3, 4.

[16] Poirer, *The Williamsburg Public Armory: A Historical Study, Block 10, Building 22F*, Colonial Williamsburg Foundation Library Research Report Series, 406, 21-22.

were particularly impacted by the removal of the government from Williamsburg as the once steady flow of travelers to Williamsburg shifted to Richmond.

Archibald Cary placed an announcement in the newspaper in late March on behalf of the government declaring that, "*the business of government, in the executive department, will cease to be transacted at Williamsburg from the 7th of April next, and will commence at Richmond on the 24th of the same month.*"[17]

Some in the government simply refused to go. Benjamin Waller, judge of the admiralty court, was one such official. This prompted the General Assembly (when it convened in May) to allow the admiralty court to continue to meet in Williamsburg.[18] The Council of State also had trouble reaching a quorum because so many of its members were reluctant to go to Richmond.[19] Others involved with the government, such as the commonwealth printers, John Clarkson and Augustine Davis, requested more time from the government to move their operation from Williamsburg to Richmond because they could not find an appropriate building in the new capital to accommodate their printing operation.[20]

Governor Jefferson, who was in Richmond by April 12, pressed forward and the General Assembly convened in Richmond on May 1, 1780. Before the month was over, news from South Carolina rocked Virginia and brought the war much closer to home.

---

[17] Dixon and Nicolson, "March 25, 1780," *Virginia Gazette*, 3.
[18] Selby, *Virginia in the Revolution*, 247.
[19] Ibid, 246.
[20] Harry M. Ward and Harold E. Greer, Jr., *Richmond during the Revolution, 1775-83*, (Charlottesville: University Press of Virginia, 1977), 41.

The War Draws Closer to Virginia

For weeks, a large British army under General Henry Clinton had besieged Charleston, South Carolina. The remnants of most of Virginia's continental line, nearly 2,000 continental troops, helped defend the city under General Benjamin Lincoln. On May 12, Lincoln surrendered the city and his army to the British.

The southern focus of the war, which began with the fall of Savannah to the British in late 1778, intensified with the fall of Charleston. A detachment of Virginia reinforcements on the march to Charleston was decimated by the British at the Waxhaws in late May and a re-constituted American southern army, which included both militia and state troops from Virginia, was routed again in August at Camden, South Carolina. With Georgia and South Carolina firmly in British hands, it appeared that North Carolina and Virginia would soon be next.

The arrival of approximately 2,200 British and German and provincial (loyalist American) troops under General Alexander Leslie on October 20, 1780, confirmed this fear. Six powerful warships escorted the transports that sailed into Hampton Roads with Leslie's troops. They landed at both Portsmouth and Newport News. General Leslie led a detachment of troops from Newport News into Hampton where he learned about Major Patrick Ferguson's stunning defeat at Kings Mountain in South Carolina just two weeks earlier.

Approximately 1,000 frontiersmen from the Carolinas and Virginia had crushed an equal number of British provincial troops under Major Ferguson and in doing so, disrupted General Charles Cornwallis's plan to conquer North Carolina. Ferguson was supposed to protect the left flank of Cornwallis's army as it marched into North Carolina while Leslie's presence in Virginia prevented Virginian reinforcements from marching south to help resist Cornwallis. With Ferguson's force destroyed, General Leslie assumed that Cornwallis's plans had changed, so he concentrated his force in Portsmouth and waited for instructions.

Governor Jefferson initially called out 10,000 militia from the southeastern counties of the commonwealth, but reduced that number to 4,150 (as well as approximately 1,000 eighteen-month continentals) once an accurate estimate of Leslie's force was made.[21] General Thomas Nelson of Yorktown commanded the militia that formed on the north side of the James River (including those assembled in Williamsburg) and General Peter Muhlenberg, a continental brigadier-general, commanded the militia and continental troops that assembled near Smithfield on the south side of the James River.[22]

A critical shortage of weapons and equipment left Virginia's forces with limited capability, so they kept their distance from General Leslie in Portsmouth. Luckily for the Virginians, General Leslie remained inexplicably inactive in Portsmouth.

Leslie's inactivity did not prevent Governor Jefferson from ordering the removal of 800 British prisoners of war in Charlottesville to Fort Frederick, Maryland in western Maryland.[23] They were part of the convention prisoners captured at Saratoga in 1777 and had just begun their fourth year of captivity, half of which occurred in Massachusetts and the other half in Virginia.

---

[21] Julian P. Boyd, ed., "Steps to be Taken to Repel General Leslie's Army, October 22, 1780," *The Papers of Thomas Jefferson*, Vol. 4, (Princeton, NJ: Princeton University Press, 1951), 61-63.

[22] Boyd, ed., "Governor Jefferson to Edward Stevens, November 10, 1780," *The Papers of Thomas Jefferson*, Vol. 4, 111

[23] Boyd, ed., "Thomas Jefferson to Samuel Huntington, November 3, 1780," *The Papers of Thomas Jefferson*, Vol. 4, 92-93.

General Leslie's inactivity perplexed Jefferson, who speculated correctly that the British loss at Kings Mountain had altered their original plans. On November 9, General Leslie finally received orders from General Cornwallis to abandon Portsmouth and sail to North Carolina to cooperate with him in the Carolinas. It took nearly two weeks for Leslie to sail out to sea, but when he did, Virginia was once again free of the enemy.

General Henry Clinton, the overall British commander in New York, was displeased with General Leslie's conduct, particularly his lack of effort to disrupt Virginia supply system. He commented in his writings after the war that he was,

> *Fully sensible of the great advantage likely to arise from possessing a naval station* [in Virginia] *and from pursuing my original plan of striking at the enemy depots at Petersburg and Richmond….*[24]

Clinton was determined to carry out his plans for Virginia and organized a new British expedition in December to do so.

Arnold's Expedition in Virginia: 1781

This new British force meant for Virginia was smaller than General Leslie's expedition, numbering just 1,800 men.[25] The commander of the expedition was a fascinating choice, newly appointed brigadier-general Benedict Arnold, the notorious American traitor. Arnold had been one of America's greatest field commanders in the first half of the war, but he betrayed

---

[24] William B. Wilcox, ed., *The American Rebellion: Sir Henry Clinton's Narrative of His Campaigns, 1775-1782*, Vol. 2, (New Haven: Yale University Press, 1954), 234.

[25] "Embarkation Return for the Following Corps, December 11, 1780," New York," *Sir Henry Clinton Papers*, 113:15, University of Michigan, William L. Clements Library.

the American cause in September 1780 while commanding the American garrison at West Point, on the Hudson River in New York, and fled to the enemy, who honored their offer of money and a commission in the British army.

Over twenty transport ships, escorted by five British warships and several privateers, carried Arnold's force to Virginia in late December.[26] A violent winter storm scattered the fleet, driving some of the transports far out to sea, so when Arnold reached Virginia at the very end of December, his force numbered just 1,200 men.

Undeterred, Arnold pressed up the James River, landing troops at Newport News and marching to Hampton to find river pilots to assist him.[27] Arnold sent troops ashore at Warwick on New Year's Eve; they skirmished with local militia the following day, but then returned to their ships to continue up the river.[28]

By January 2, Arnold reached Burwell's Ferry, which lay on the north bank of the river just four miles from Williamsburg. The former capital fell into a state of panic at the news of Arnold's arrival. William Tatham was sent to Williamsburg by General Friedrich von Steuben, the ranking continental general in Virginia. He carried a message for General Thomas Nelson, who commanded Virginia's militia in the field. Tatham recalled that, "*On my arrival* [in Williamsburg] *I found the Town in confusion, and the inhabitants alarmed by the expectation of an immediate*

---

[26] Joseph Tustin, ed., *Diary of the American War: A Hessian Journal*, (New Haven: Yale University Press, 1979), 258,
[27] John K. Laughton, ed., *The Journal of Rear-Admiral Bartholomew James*, (London: Navy Records Society, 1896), 94.
[28] Tustin, ed., *Diary of the American War: A Hessian Journal*, 259-260.

engagement at Kings Mill...."[29] Tatham rode on to Kings Mill, which was adjacent to Burwell's Ferry, and found,

> *General Nelson and...Colo. James Innis at the head of about fifty five men, under the more immediate command of a Major Harrod, waiting to give the Enemy battle as they landed; and most of the Enemy's Ships were come to an anchor off the Place, a small boat taking the Soundings towards the Shore, and larger boats filled with men and maneuvering towards the land in readiness for debarkation.*[30]

Nathanael Burwell, the owner of the ferry crossing on the James River, was also with the militia and reported to Governor Jefferson that they numbered under two hundred, still far fewer than was needed to resist Arnold's force.

> *The Enemy's Fleet have just now* [arrived] *off this Place; they consist of 23 Sail, including two Men of war; a number of Flat bottom'd Boats are a-Stern of the Ships full of men. We have near 200 men under the Command of Colo. Innis and myself, a number insufficient for the present Purpose: however nothing shall be wanting as far as we're able to oppose the Enemy if they attempt to land. A Small Party of Foot and Horse are now engag'd with a Boat detachd from the Fleet.*[31]

---

[29] Boyd, ed., "William Tatham to William Armistead Burwell, June 13, 1805," *The Papers of Thomas Jefferson*, Vol. 4, 274.
[30] Ibid.
[31] Boyd, ed., "Nathaniel Burwell to Governor Jefferson, January 2, 1781," *The Papers of Thomas Jefferson*, Vol. 4, 294.

From Arnold's vantage point on the river, it was difficult to judge the size of the militia gathered on shore. Captain Johann Ewald, the commander of a detachment of German jagers (riflemen) believed that there were several battalions of militia formed along the shore.[32] Arnold opted not to engage the militia directly, but instead, sent a flag of truce ashore with a message that he hoped would intimidate the militia into submission. Arnold declared in his note that,

> *Having the honor to command a Body of His Majesty's Troops, sent for the protection of his Loyal Subjects in this country, I am surprised to observe the hostile appearance of the Inhabitants under Arms on the Shore. I have therefore sent Lieut. White, with a Flagg of Truce, to be informed of their intentions. If they are to offer a vain opposition to the Troops under my command, in their landing, they must be answerable for the consequences.*[33]

Asserting that he had, "*not the least intention to injure the peaceable Inhabitants in their persons or property,*" Arnold pledged that whatever provision the inhabitants willingly supplied his force, "*shall be punctually paid for.*"[34]

General Nelson rejected Arnold's offer, declaring that he, "*would not and could not give up to a traitor.*"[35] Furthermore, continued Nelson, he declared that, "*if he were to get hold of*

---

[32] Tustin, ed., *Diary of the American War: A Hessian Journal*, 260.
[33] Michael Kranish, "General Arnold to the Officer Commanding the Party on Shore, January 2, 1781," *Flight from Monticello: Thomas Jefferson at War*, (Oxford: Oxford University Press, 2010), 173.
[34] Ibid.
[35] Tustin, ed., *Diary of the American War: A Hessian Journal*, 260-261.

Arnold, he would hang him up by the heels, according to the orders of Congress."[36]

Arnold chose not to push the matter and sailed further up the river, anchoring off Jamestown Island at nightfall. In the morning, he ordered his troops ashore, but reversed himself just as they reached shore and recalled them to the transports. Captain Ewald believed that, "*news that a strong corps of Virginia militia had assembled*," in Williamsburg, was the likely reason Arnold changed his mind and continued further up the James River.[37] Another possible reason for the change in plans was that the wind, which had been unfavorable the day before for moving up the river shifted and blew upriver in the morning. With both the wind and tide in his favor, Arnold continued upriver to his true destination, Richmond.[38]

While Arnold and his fleet pressed upriver, brushing aside what little resistance was offered by Virginia's disorganized forces, Governor Jefferson and General Nelson scrambled to respond. Nelson reported to Governor Jefferson on the evening of January 4, that he was at Byrd's Tavern (on the James City County-New Kent County line) with his force of militia and that he expected to rendezvous with militia from several counties shortly as they proceeded up the peninsula towards Richmond.[39]

Arnold easily out paced General Nelson to Richmond and entered Virginia's capital on January 5. Once again, little resistance was offered the British and they were able to destroy an important foundry just upriver from Richmond as well as

---

[36] Ibid.
[37] Ibid, 261.
[38] Boyd, ed., "II. Arnold's Invasion as Reported by Jefferson in the Virginia Gazette, Richmond, January 13, 1781," *The Papers of Thomas Jefferson*, Vol. 4, 269.
[39] Boyd, ed., "Thomas Nelson to Governor Jefferson, January 4, 1781," *The Papers of Thomas Jefferson*, Vol. 4, 307.

several warehouses and public storehouses and a smith's shop (probably James Anderson's) along with additional items of military value.[40]

By January 10, Arnold and his men, reinforced by the missing troop transports that had finally arrived, started back down the James River. General Steuben, anticipating that Arnold might still stop at Williamsburg, where General Nelson had four hundred militia assembled, ordered over five hundred additional militia who were marching to join him on the south side of the James River, to cross the river and march to Williamsburg instead.[41]

Arnold's fleet reached Cobham, across from Jamestown Island, on January 12, but much to the relief of the inhabitants of Williamsburg, showed no interest towards the north side of the river. General Nelson reported to Governor Jefferson on January 13, that the enemy had passed Burwell's Ferry. "*I think they intend nothing further on the North Side of James River at present*," noted Nelson.[42]

General Nelson was correct, Benedict Arnold had completed the first part of his expedition, a swift strike at Virginia's capital to disrupt the commonwealth's war effort. It was now time to establish a secure British post in Portsmouth that would continue to disrupt Virginia's war effort and serve for future British operations in the Old Dominion.

With the worst of Arnold's raid seemingly over, Governor Jefferson instructed General Nelson to discharge some of the militia gathered in Williamsburg. "*As I suppose by this time*

---

[40] Davies, ed., "General Arnold to General Clinton, January 21, 1781," *Documents of the American Revolution*, Vol. 20, 41.

[41] Richard K. Showman, ed., "Baron Steuben to General Greene, January 11, 1781," *The Papers of General Nathanael Greene*, Vol. 7. (Chapel Hill: The University of North Carolina Press, 1994), 98.

[42] Boyd, ed., "Thomas Nelson to Governor Jefferson, January 13, 1781," *The Papers of Thomas Jefferson*, Vol. 4, 351.

you may have more Men than Arms," wrote Jefferson on January 15, "*and there are no more Arms fit for use remaining in the public Stock, economy will require that the surplus Militia be discharged.*"[43] General Nelson confirmed Jefferson's assumption about a shortage of weapons the following day, reporting that he had about one thousand militia in Williamsburg, some who were not armed and would thus be discharged.[44] It is likely that they were quartered in the barracks behind the former governor's palace. Such relatively` comfortable quarters, however, did not alleviate the desire of most of the militia to return to their homes.

General Nelson urged Governor Jefferson to call the General Assembly back into session to address the significant troop shortage Virginia faced due in large part from the reluctance of so many militia to serve in the field any longer.

> *From disagreeable Experience I am convinced that the Defense of this Country must not rest on the Militia under its present Establishment. They have been so much harassed lately that they would give nearly half they possess to raise Regulars, rather than be subject to the Distresses they feel at leaving their Plantations and Families. We have been obliged to call out the whole of the Militia from several Counties, some of whom I have not been able to discharge for Want of Men to relieve them. I am order'd by Baron Steuben to keep in this Neck 1,000 or 1,200 Men, and were I to discharge the Men who were on Duty the last Invasion* [when General Leslie arrived in October of the

---

[43] Boyd, ed., "Governor Jefferson to Thomas Nelson, January 15, 1781," *The Papers of Thomas Jefferson*, Vol. 4, 371.

[44] Boyd, ed., "Thomas Nelson to Governor Jefferson, January 16, 1781," *The Papers of Thomas Jefferson*, Vol. 4, 383.

> previous year] *which I confess they have a Right to claim, I should not have one third of that Number.*[45]

While Virginia's leaders struggled to raise an adequate force to defend against further incursions by the British, Arnold ordered the construction of earthworks around Portsmouth and established two important posts at Kemp's Landing and Great Bridge to secure adequate forage and provision for his force. Arnold's troops skirmished frequently with small parties of militia in Princess Anne County and kept watch on General Peter Muhlenberg's force of over 1,000 militia posted 25 miles to the southwest of Portsmouth near Suffolk.[46]

In mid-February, a small French naval squadron of three powerful warships sailed into Hampton Roads. General Nelson rode from Williamsburg to Hampton upon word of their arrival and met the French commander, Captain Arnaud de Gardeur de Tilly aboard his ship. He was disappointed to learn that their stay would be brief and that they intended to cruise off the Virginia Capes until the Virginians were better prepared to cooperate with them on an attack upon Portsmouth.[47]

Nelson lamented to Governor Jefferson the following day, February 19, that upon the departure of the French ships, "*the Enemy will be left at Liberty to make use of all the Advantages which their Command of the Water gives them over us.*"[48] He

---

[45] Boyd, ed., "Thomas Nelson to Governor Jefferson, January 22, 1781," *The Papers of Thomas Jefferson*, Vol. 4, 427.

[46] Henry Muhlenberg, "General Muhlenberg to General Greene, February 24, 1781," *The Life of Major-General Peter Muhlenberg*, (Philadelphia: Cary and Hart, 1849), 389-390.

[47] Boyd, ed., "Thomas Nelson to Governor Jefferson, February 18, 1781," *The Papers of Thomas Jefferson*, Vol. 4, 650.

[48] Boyd, ed., "Thomas Nelson to Governor Jefferson, February 19, 1781," *The Papers of Thomas Jefferson*, Vol. 4, 658.

was particularly concerned about Hampton and Newport News and declared to the governor that,

> *It gives me the utmost Pain that I find myself unable to give them the Protection they merit; the Force at present under my Command* [on the peninsula] *amounting to not more than four hundred Effectives. The Militia from Albemarle and Fluvanna are much distressed for Want of clothing, and ought to be relieved if it can be done.*[49]

General Nelson added that he had requested from the French commander any arms and military stores he might spare and hoped the governor would not disapprove of such a request.[50]

Two days after this message, Colonel James Innes, writing on behalf of General Nelson, who had fallen ill, provided a detailed description of the poor condition of the militia posted in Williamsburg.

> *The present distressed Situation of the militia, under my Command induces me, to address your Excellency on their behalf. Most of them are totally destitute of the necessary cloathing to protect them from the Inclemency of the weather. They are lousy, dirty and ragged, and from those Circumstances becoming every day more sickly. In addition to this, such a spirit of disquietude prevails among the poorer Class, whose...Labours are necessary to sustain their families, that I have been, and still am apprehensive of a mutiny, unless some assurances can be given of a*

---

[49] Ibid, 659.
[50] Ibid.

> *speedy relief.... I have prevailed on the troops to wait patiently your Excellencys Answer....*[51]

One hundred and fifty miles to the west, the re-built American southern army, reinforced by Virginia militia from the west and under the command of General Nathanael Greene of Rhode Island, crossed the Dan River back into North Carolina to pursue General Cornwallis and his two thousand man British army that had pursued Greene for the last month through North Carolina. This reversal of roles triggered a month of maneuvering between the two armies that led to a bloody and significant clash at Guilford Courthouse in mid-March.

A small engagement also occurred in mid-March on the western edge of Portsmouth when General Muhlenberg, accompanied by General Marquis de Lafayette (who had passed through Williamsburg on March 16 before crossing the James River to join Muhlenberg) probed Benedict Arnold's lines at Portsmouth.[52] General Lafayette arrived in Virginia ahead of his one thousand man continental light infantry corps, which General Washington had sent to Virginia to assist the commonwealth. These troops, perhaps the best soldiers in the American army, were expected to arrive soon and when they did, Lafayette planned to use them in conjunction with Virginia's forces and the French navy to capture General Arnold and his entire force at Portsmouth.

Alas, a powerful British naval squadron of warships arrived in Hampton Roads ahead of Lafayette's light infantry

---

[51] Boyd, ed., "James Innes to Governor Jefferson, February 21, 1781," *The Papers of Thomas Jefferson*, Vol. 4, 675.

[52] Julian P. Boyd, ed., "General LaFayette to Governor Jefferson, March 16, 1781," *The Papers of Thomas Jefferson*, Vol. 5 (Princeton, NJ: Princeton University Press, 1952), 159-160.

and the French navy and when a second fleet of British transport ships arrived with nearly 2,500 troops under General William Phillips, all hope of capturing Benedict Arnold in Portsmouth vanished.[53]

General Lafayette halted his troop movement southward and prepared to return to Washington's main army in New York while General Muhlenberg withdrew from the outskirts of Portsmouth back to Suffolk.

In Williamsburg, General Steuben, joined by General George Weedon of Fredericksburg, a former continental general who had resigned from the army in protest over rank in 1778, also scrambled to adjust to the arrival of British reinforcements. Weedon had assumed command of the militia in Williamsburg while General Nelson recovered from his illness and then attended the General Assembly in Richmond. Weedon reported to Jefferson on March 28, that with the agreement of both General Lafayette and General Steuben, who met with Weedon in Williamsburg, he had withdrawn the troops posted below Williamsburg because there were too few there to, "*cover the Country from* [Williamsburg] *to Hampton*."[54] Weedon added,

> *I have the honour to transmit to your Excellency a Copy of a General Return, by which you will see how inadequate the Strength of the Troops, under my Command, must be to the Service expected from them.... Only Caroline and Spotsylvania* [County] *have sent any men; indeed I cannot see how the Country is to be defended, when a Call of the Executive is paid as little regard to as it would be from*

---

[53] Boyd, ed., "George Weedon to Governor Jefferson, March 28, 1781," *The Papers of Thomas Jefferson*, Vol. 5, 273.
[54] Ibid.

> *those no way in Authority; and indeed those few that come into the Field, only remain as long as they please, and then go back, some with their Officers at their heads, without consulting the Service or the Officer commanding.*[55]

Three days later, Weedon informed Governor Jefferson of a British landing at Newport News.

> [The enemy] *embark'd 700 Men, crossed over to Newport News with an evident intention of beating up our Troops at the Halfway House. They finding them withdrawn, Secretly and silently returned, giving out their expedition was intended against Williamsburg but failed in consequence of being lost and not landing before day.*[56]

Weedon added that,

> *In consequence of drawing the Troops from below the People murmur exceedingly, and threaten to make their Terms with the Enemy. I am sending down a Detachment for the sake of contentment, but it will not afford Cover to the Country or render any security more than giving Countenance to the People. The Officer will be order'd to change his Ground often and to act as a party of observation. I am exceedingly distress'd for Arms and Accoutrements having several*

---

[55] Ibid.

[56] Boyd, ed., "George Weedon to Governor Jefferson, April 1, 1781," *The Papers of Thomas Jefferson*, Vol. 5, 317.

> *of the few Men under my Command without anything of the sort in their Hands.*[57]

Virginia's leaders speculated in early April that the British reinforcements in Portsmouth under General William Phillips might be intended to support General Cornwallis in North Carolina. If so, it would be necessary, urged Generals Weedon and Steuben, to send reinforcements to General Greene.[58] Just where these troops would come from and how they would be properly supplied was anyone's guess, but the belief, and perhaps hope, was that the bulk of the British troops in Virginia would soon head south, leaving General Arnold to maintain the British post in Portsmouth. This assumption was soon proved wrong.

---

[57] Ibid.

[58] Boyd, ed., "George Weedon to Governor Jefferson, April 3, 1781," and "General Steuben to Governor Jefferson, April 4, 1781," *The Papers of Thomas Jefferson*, Vol. 5, 338, 349-350.

Seven

The Virginia Campaign: 1781

On April 18, over two thousand British troops under General Phillips sailed out of Portsmouth and up the James River. Their destination was Williamsburg, where Phillips hoped to surprise a body of militia in Virginia's former capital.[1] There would be no surprise for the Virginians; Colonel James Innes commanded the militia posted at Williamsburg and he learned of the British approach up the river in the late afternoon of their departure. He sent an express to Richmond to inform Governor Jefferson of the situation.

> *I have this Moment received by express from Captain Kelly, stationed a little above Newport News, an Account that eleven Vessels, chiefly Square rigged, have turned Newport News Point on their Way up the River. His Letter bears Date at 10 this Morning, so that, the Wind being fresh at South East, they could with Ease reach Burwell's Ferry this Evening. I am making the best Disposition to receive them, and have ordered the Stores to be removed from this Place.*[2]

Governor Jefferson received the news early the next morning and called for the militia from counties near Richmond

---

[1] Lt. Col. John Simcoe, *A Journal of the Operations of the Queen's Rangers, from the end of the year 1777 to the Conclusion of the Late American War*, (1789), 131.
[2] Boyd, ed., "James Innes to Governor Jefferson, April 18, 1781," *The Papers of Thomas Jefferson*, Vol. 5, 489.

and Petersburg to muster at those two locations.[3] On the morning of April 20, Innes, still in Williamsburg, informed Governor Jefferson that

> *Fourteen flatt bottomed Boats, a ship, two brigs, two sloops, and one schooner heavily manned, have just arrived at Burwell's Ferry. From every appearance I think they mean to land, as they have halted with a favorable Tide. I believe they wait for nothing but the arrival of two schooners which have their Cavalry on board.... I moved out all the stores at this post last Evening.*[4]

General Phillips sent a large force ashore that same day. Lieutenant Colonel John Simcoe led the assault. He commanded the Queen's Rangers, a provincial force made up of Americans loyal to the British crown. Simcoe observed that, "t*he enemy had thrown up entrenchments to secure* [against a] *landing* [at Burwell's Ferry] *and these appeared to be fully manned.*"[5] Nevertheless, General Phillips sent Simcoe and his rangers ashore.

Escorted by one lone gunboat with a six pound cannon upon its bow, Simcoe's force was rowed ashore in longboats. About half way to shore, the longboats suddenly swung hard right, the sailors and soldiers in them rowing furiously downriver toward a creek a mile below Burwell's Ferry. The gunboat remained off the ferry landing and raked the shore with

---

[3] Boyd, ed., "Governor Jefferson to the County Lieutenants of Henrico and Certain Other Counties, April 19, 1781," *The Papers of Thomas Jefferson*, Vol. 5, 496.

[4] Boyd, ed., "James Innes to Governor Jefferson, April 20, 1781," *The Papers of Thomas Jefferson*, Vol. 5, 504-505.

[5] Simcoe, *A Journal of the Operations of the Queen's Rangers*, 132,

cannon fire to dissuade the militia at Burwell's from leaving their entrenchments to redeploy downriver. Simcoe's force thus landed unopposed and without loss.[6]

With their entrenchments flanked and the main force of General Phillips still to come ashore, the militia at Burwell's Ferry abandoned their post and withdrew to Williamsburg, just four miles inland. Reports of another British force landing further up the river near Jamestown Island convinced Colonel Innes that General Phillips meant to entrap him in Williamsburg. He ordered the militia to withdraw northward up the New Kent Road. They halted at Allen's Ordinary, six miles from Williamsburg, where Innes wrote to Governor Jefferson to explain his actions.

> *This Day at two o' clock, the Enemy attempted and made good their Landing at Burwell's Ferry. At the same time several armed vessels and 16 flatt bottomed Boats proceeded up to James Town where I have been informed they have since Landed. As soon as I found the Designs of the Enemy to circumvent me, I moved the troops to this place which is the nearest to the Town that can be taken with safety while the Enemy are masters of the water. There was some slight skirmishing between the advance of the Enemy and our Guards of observation at Burwell's ferry. We have sustained no loss. All our Guards have joined the main Body. By several persons Just from Williamsburg I am informed that the british troops were a mile from the Town. Some Hospital stores, and fifteen sick men unable to move and some stores belonging to the Commissary's Department...I have*

[6] Ibid, 131-133.

> *been obliged to leave behind me. The Troops under my Command are extremely harassed having laid upon their arms for upwards of fifty hours during such time they have received no Sustinance.... We suffer extremely for want of provision.*[7]

Colonel Innes updated Governor Jefferson the following day, providing more detail.

> *About 3 oClock Yesterday the Enemy landed at Burwell's Ferry 500 Infantry, 50 Horse and 4 Pieces Artillery, which with a seeming Intention of landing in force at Jamestown or on some part of the River above us, obliged us to evacuate the Town and move up to Allens Ordinarly six Miles above. Major Armistead with 150 Men and Capt. Kelly with 50 Riflemen were ordered down and had a skirmish with the Enemy which terminated in our favour.*[8]

This skirmish was likely the one described by Dr. Robert Honyman in a journal he kept of the war. Although not an eyewitness nor even a resident of Williamsburg, Honyman was a reliable source on events that occurred in Virginia during the war, often turning to General Thomas Nelson and other participants for first hand information.[9]

---

[7] Boyd, ed., "James Innes to Governor Jefferson, April 20, 1781," *The Papers of Thomas Jefferson*, Vol. 5, 506.
[8] Boyd, ed., "James Innes to Governor Jefferson, April 21, 1781," *The Papers of Thomas Jefferson*, Vol. 5, 521.
[9] Richard K. MacMaster, ed., "The Journal of Dr. Robert Honyman, April 17 – November 25, 1781," *Virginia Magazine of History and Biography*, 79, no. 4 (October 1971), 388.

> *On Saturday morning the 21,* [Colonel Innes] *sent down a detachment to attack the enemy's picket who were posted near the college. The militia attacked them, but the enemy being reinforced, they were obliged to retreat. In this skirmish we lost 2 or 3 men.*[10]

This was apparently not the only clash that occurred in Williamsburg in April. General Samuel Graham, who was a captain in the Eightieth Regiment with General Phillips in 1781, recalled in his memoirs that a picket guard composed of some of his men posted near the college was briefly attacked by, "*a company of young men, students at the university, composing a volunteer corps, [who] managed to creep into a thicket unobserved.*"[11] The British soldiers standing guard had just left the warmth of a large fire to seek shelter from the rain when, "*a volley was fired in the direction of the blazing fire from the brushwood.*"[12] The British returned fire but neither side hit anyone and the skirmish was over within a minute.

A brief clash also occurred in Yorktown, twelve miles away, when Lieutenant Colonel Simcoe charged into town with a detachment of cavalry. It was a quick but successful raid upon the militia posted there. They were dispersed and a barracks burned without the loss of any men.[13] Simcoe then rode back to Williamsburg to join General Phillips. Another large British force under Lieutenant Colonel Robert Abercrombie landed on the Chickahominy River and destroyed the Virginia State navy

---

[10] Ibid, 393.

[11] James J. Graham, ed., *Memoir of General Samuel Graham with Notices of the Campaigns in Which he was Engaged from 1779 to 1801*, (Edinburgh: R. & R. Clark, 1862), 34.

[12] Ibid.

[13] Simcoe, *A Journal of the Operations of the Queen's Rangers*, 133.

yard there. On Sunday, April 22, General Phillips led his troops from Williamsburg towards the Chickahominy where his ships waited to take them further up the river.[14]

Williamsburg emerged from its first visit of enemy troops relatively unscathed. Dr. Honyman noted that there were only three to four hundred British troops in Williamsburg with General Phillips and General Arnold and that, "*While they remained in Williamsburgh they behaved with the greatest moderation & even politeness.*"[15] It is unclear, but doubtful that General Phillip's moderation and politeness extended to such public property as Anderson's armory or the barracks behind the old governor's residence. Both were in ruins by September when American and French troops arrived in Williamsburg, but they could have been destroyed in a second "visit" of the British army in June.[16]

General Phillips himself hinted that he had destroyed public stores in Williamsburg in a later April letter to Governor Jefferson discussing the conduct of both sides.

> *It is a principle of the British army engaged in the present war, which they esteem as an unfortunate one, to conduct it with every attention to humanity and the laws of war; and in the necessary destruction of public stores of every kind, to prevent, as far as possible, that of private property. I call upon the inhabitants of Yorktown, Williamsburg, Petersburg, and*

---

[14] Ibid, 134.

[15] MacMaster, ed., "The Journal of Dr. Robert Honyman, April 17 – November 25, 1781," *Virginia Magazine of History and Biography*, 79, no. 4, 392.

[16] Poirer, *The Williamsburg Public Armory: A Historical Study, Block 10, Building 22F,* Colonial Williamsburg Foundation Library Research Report Series, 406, 23-24.

> *Chesterfield, for a proof of the mild treatment they have received from the king's troops....*[17]

One wonders if General Phillips's reluctance to strike at private property extended to accepting or seizing runaway slaves who fled to the British upon their arrival in Williamsburg. Thousands of slaves did run to the British in 1781 seeking their freedom, but whether they did so in Williamsburg in April or later in the year when the British returned in June under General Charles Cornwallis, is unclear.

One thing is clear and that is that by June, an enormous number of enslaved people followed the British army. Captain Ewald, who returned to the army to resume command of his jaegers (riflemen) in June once he recovered from a wound suffered in the spring, observed in his journal that the army under General Cornwallis looked like, "*a wandering Arabian or Tartar horde*," because of all the seized horses and runaway slaves that were with the army.[18] He recalled that,

> *Every officer had four to six horses and three or four Negroes.... Yes indeed, I can testify that every soldier had his Negro, who carried his provisions and bundles. This multitude always hunted at a gallop, and behind the baggage followed well over four thousand Negroes of both sexes and all ages. Any place this horde approached was eaten clean, like an acre invaded by a swarm of locusts. Where all these people lived was a riddle to me. Fortunately, the army*

---

[17] Boyd, ed., "General Phillips to Governor Jefferson, April 28, 1781," *The Papers of Thomas Jefferson*, Vol. 5, 69.

[18] Tustin, ed., *Diary of the American War: A Hessian Journal*, 305.

seldom stayed in one place longer than a day or a night.[19]

It is unclear whether General Phillips encouraged or allowed such activity in the army during the six weeks he commanded it, but it is certain that General Cornwallis did once he arrived in Virginia in mid-May.

Forces Converge on Virginia

In the immediate aftermath of the British army's first "visit' to Williamsburg since the war began, the city's inhabitants must have felt some relief at the little damage or disruption inflicted on the city. The principle public buildings were spared and it appears there was little in the way of plunder seized.

Phillips and his force moved on to Petersburg just days after they left Williamsburg, where they clashed with militia under General Muhlenberg. They continued north and destroyed the continental camp at Chesterfield Courthouse and the Virginia State navy at Osborne's Landing, but left Richmond alone when General Lafayette and his continental light infantry arrived.

Phillips started back down the James River, but reversed himself and encamped at Petersburg, where he fell gravely ill and died in mid-May. A few days after his death, General Cornwallis arrived with the remnants of his army (about 1,500 men) from North Carolina. Another British reinforcement from New York sailed into Portsmouth in May and just like that, the British had approximately seven thousand troops in the Old Dominion.

---

[19] Ibid.

General Lafayette's continental light infantry and the Virginia militia were no match for the British, so Lafayette, the ranking American officer in Virginia, wisely kept his distance from Cornwallis, refusing to engage him in battle. After a long pursuit of Lafayette, and raids upon Charlottesville, where Virginia's legislature had fled, and Point of Fork on the James River, where an important supply depot sat, General Cornwallis headed east towards Williamsburg. Lafayette, reinforced by approximately eight hundred Pennsylvania continentals under General Anthony Wayne, trailed Cornwallis and even sent a detachment after the British rearguard. The Americans caught them foraging near Spencer's Ordinary, just a few miles outside of Williamsburg on June 26, and a clash ensued.

Battle of Spencer's Ordinary

Lieutenant Colonel Simcoe of the Queen's Rangers commanded the British rearguard at Spencer's Ordinary. It consisted of an infantry battalion of the Rangers along with a company of British grenadiers, a company of British light infantry, a detachment of Captain Ewald's jaegers, a detachment of loyalist militia from North Carolina, one cannon and Simcoe's cavalry, altogether approximately 300 strong.[20]

Simcoe's infantry reached Spencer's Ordinary ahead of the cavalry, who trailed behind to escort cattle that had been seized on the march. While they waited along the road to Williamsburg for the cavalry to catch up, the infantry ate breakfast and rested, dreading the summer heat they knew awaited them later in the day.[21] When Simcoe arrived with the cavalry, he learned that a number of cattle were nearby and sent

[20] Tustin, ed., *Diary of the American War: A Hessian Journal*, 307-308, and Simcoe, *A Journal of the Operations of the Queen's Rangers*, 160.

[21] Tustin, ed., *Diary of the American War: A Hessian Journal*, 308.

the Tory militia to gather them while his cavalry dismounted and rested their horses.[22]

Unbeknownst to Simcoe and his men, a large American detachment under Colonel Richard Butler of Pennsylvania had marched all night in pursuit. Butler's force included a detachment of Pennsylvania Continentals, two contingents of Virginia riflemen, and fifty dragoons under Major William McPherson.[23] Most of Butler's infantry trailed behind the dragoons, but fifty of them rode double upon the horses and advanced ahead of the infantry.[24] McPherson's double mounted cavalry were the first to catch Simcoe, bursting upon the Tory militia tending to the cattle. The panicked Tories fled, but a lone trumpeter posted between the foragers and dismounted rangers distracted the Americans away from the vulnerable rangers, giving them time to remount and join the battle.[25] Simcoe proudly recalled that his cavalry commander, Captain Shank, "*led* [his horsemen] *to the charge on the enemy's flank, which was somewhat exposed…*[and] *broke them entirely*."[26] Major McPherson was unhorsed in the clash and his dragoons scattered in all directions. Fortunately for the Americans, their infantry arrived in time to take up the fight.

At the sound of gunfire, Lieutenant Colonel Simcoe, who was with the infantry at Spencer's Ordinary, raced towards his cavalry to investigate. He ordered the baggage wagons and cattle to immediately proceed to Williamsburg and sent a dispatch to General Cornwallis informing him of the attack.[27]

---

[22] Simcoe, *A Journal of the Operations of the Queen's Rangers,* 160.
[23] Henry Lee, *The Revolutionary War Memoirs of General Henry* Lee, (New York: Da Capo Press, 1998), 429-430.
[24] Ibid, 430.
[25] Simcoe, *A Journal of the Operations of the Queen's Rangers,* 160-161.
[26] Ibid, 161.
[27] Simcoe, *A Journal of the Operations of the Queen's Rangers,* 162,

Simcoe witnessed his cavalry repulse the American horsemen, but then saw them equally repulsed by American infantry posted in a thick wood. While he worked to reorganize his cavalry, Captain Ewald led the infantry against the bulk of the American infantry, which had deployed in the woods just to the north of Spencer's Ordinary and the road to Williamsburg. Ewald formed most of the infantry upon a ploughed field and orchard facing the woods and ordered them straight at the Americans while he sent his jaegers to the right to circle around the American left flank and attack them from the rear.[28] Ewald led the movement forward and recalled that

> *I called to Lieutenant Bickell to...fall upon the enemy's left flank and rear with all the jagers. At that instant, I jumped off my horse and placed myself in front of the center of the grenadiers and light infantry company. I asked them not to fire a shot, but to attack with the bayonet... The enemy, who had moved forward, was taken aback by our advance.* [They] *waited for us up to forty paces, fired a volley, killed two thirds of the grenadiers, and withdrew... We came among them and engaged them hand to hand. The enemy now came under rifle fire from the jagers on his flank and rear, and hurried to escape. We captured a French officer, a captain of riflemen, and twenty-two men, partly from the so-called Wild Irish Riflemen, and partly from the light infantry.*[29]

With the Americans repulsed and his baggage and cattle safely enroute to Williamsburg, Simcoe disengaged his troops

---

[28] Tustin, ed., *Diary of the American War: A Hessian Journal*, 308-309.
[29] Tustin, ed., *Diary of the American War: A Hessian Journal*, 309.

and resumed his march to Williamsburg. As he had sent all the baggage wagons to Williamsburg at the start of the fight, there was no way to transport his wounded, so he left them at Spencer's Ordinary under a flag of truce. About two milcs into his march to Williamsburg, Simcoe met General Cornwallis with a large reinforcement, and together they returned to retrieve the wounded.[30]

Both sides claimed victory at Spencer's Ordinary and the losses were nearly equal. Lieutenant-Colonel Simcoe reported eleven men killed and twenty-five wounded but Captain Ewald put the total losses closer to sixty.[31] Lieutenant Colonel Butler reported thirty-three casualties after the battle, far fewer than the enemy believed they inflicted.[32] The British returned to Williamsburg with their wounded while Colonel Butler rejoined General Lafayette and his army at Tyree's Plantation, twenty miles northwest of Williamsburg.[33] The Americans remained a day's march from Williamsburg for over a week, waiting for General Cornwallis to make his next move. During that time the British commander and his army encamped in and around Williamsburg.

The British Occupation of Williamsburg

General Cornwallis used the residence of Reverend James Madison, president of the college of William and Mary, as his

---

[30] Simcoe, *A Journal of the Operations of the Queen's Rangers,* 165-166.
[31] Simcoe, *A Journal of the Operations of the Queen's Rangers,* 165, and Tustin, ed., *Diary of the American War: A Hessian Journal*, 312.
[32] Henry P. Johnston, "Appendix 15, Return of the Killed, Wounded, and Missing of the Light Corps under Colonel Butler, in the Action of the 26th of June, 1781," *The Yorktown Campaign and the Surrender of Cornwallis, 1781*, (1881: Ft. Washington, PA: Eastern National, 1997), 190.
[33] Stanley J. Idzerda, ed., "General LaFayette to General Greene, June 27, 1781," *LaFayette in the Age of the American Revolution: Selected Letters and Papers, 1776-1790*, Vol. 4, (Ithaca and London: Cornell University Press, 1981), 216.

residence and headquarters.[34] St. George Tucker, who returned to Williamsburg a week after the British departed in early July, wrote to his wife that,

> *Our friend Mr. Madison and his Lady...Were turned out of their house to make room for Lord Cornwallis. Happily the college afforded them an asylum. They were refused the small privilege of drawing water from their own well. A contemptuous treatment, with the danger of starving, were the only evils which he recounted, as none of his servants left him.*[35]

The arrival of the British army in Williamsburg provided an opportunity for many enslaved people to escape their bondage. Although it appears that none of Reverend Madison's slaves fled, Tucker reported that others, such as those held by James McClurg, a professor at the college, did. It was not an easy choice to make because there was no assurance of success. The British army did not guarantee freedom to those who fled, they just allowed them to follow the army. If Britain was victorious in the dispute with America, then there was a very good chance for freedom for those who fled, but if America prevailed, the outcome would likely be dire.

Tucker did not consider the plight of the escaped slaves in his description of the British occupation, he focused on the impact their flight had on those they fled from.

---

[34] John Austen Stevens, ed., "The Southern Campaign, 1781: From Guildford Courthouse to the Siege of York: Narrated in the Letters from Judge St George Tucker to his Wife, July 11, 1781," *The Magazine of American History*, Vol. 7, (July, 1881), 207.
[35] Ibid.

> [Mr. McClurg] *has no small servant left and but two girls. He feeds and saddles his own horse, and is a philosopher enough to enjoy the good that springs from the absence of the British, without repining at what he lost by them. Poor Mr. Cocke was deserted by his favorite man Clem; and Mrs. Cocke, by the loss of her cook, is obliged to have recourse to her neighbors to dress her dinner for her. They have but one little boy...left to wait on them within doors....*[36]

Several slaves in the household of Williamsburg's most prominent widow, Elizabeth Randolph, wife of the late speaker of the House of Burgesses, Peyton Randolph, also seized the chance for freedom and fled to the British when they arrived.[37] Tucker informed his wife that,

> *Your old friend Aunt Betty is in* [a difficult] *situation. A child of Sir Peyton Skipwith, who is with her, was deserted by its nurse; and the good old lady was left without a human being to assist her in any respect for some days.*[38]

As for the British army of nearly five thousand troops in Williamsburg, most likely encamped in tents set up throughout or on the edge of town. Field officers (colonels and above) likely found quarters in homes or

---

[36] Ibid.

[37] Raymond Townsend, *The Will of Betty Randolph," in "Peyton Randolph Historical Report, Block 28, Building 6, Lot 207 & 237*, Colonial Williamsburg Foundation Library Research Report Series 1537, 1967.

[38] Stevens, ed., "The Southern Campaign, 1781: From Guildford Courthouse to the Siege of York: Narrated in the Letters from Judge St George Tucker to his Wife, July 11, 1781," *The Magazine of American History*, Vol. 7, 207.

buildings, but the heat and humidity of a Virginia summer likely made sleeping in a tent more bearable than indoors. It is difficult to ascertain as little is documented either way.

Captain Ewald was likely not the only German or British soldier who found the summer climate of Virginia oppressive.

> *For six weeks the heat has been so unbearable that many men have been lost by sunstroke or their reason has been impaired. Everything that one has on his body is soaked as with water from the constant perspiration. The nights are especially terrible, when there is so little air that one can scarcely breathe. The torment of several billions of insects, which plagued us day and night, appears to be over now for certain.*[39]

Ever the military tactician, Ewald found that, despite the heat and insects, Williamsburg was a good location for a military camp.

> *This area is enclosed by deep ravines, which make up a kind of fortified encampment. Because of their marshy banks, both creeks can be crossed only by way of two bridges at Williamsburg, which makes this area a very good position for an army; but it must also be master of the Chesapeake Bay, so that no one can land in its rear. This was the situation with us, where we were enclosed by the splendid and excellently cultivated country between the York and James rivers.*

---

[39] Tustin, ed., *Diary of the American War: A Hessian Journal*, 314.

> *In this area, a strong army could subsist for an entire year.*[40]

St. George Tucker also noticed the swarms of flies in Williamsburg when he returned to the city in mid-July. He blamed the British for them without explanation.

> *Among the plagues the British left in Williamsburg, that of flies is inconceivable. It is impossible to eat, drink, sleep, write, sit still, or even walk about in peace on account of their confounded stings. Their numbers exceed all description....*[41]

Tucker also blamed the appearance of smallpox in the city on the British army.

> *The smallpox, which the hellish polling of these infamous wretches has spread in every place through which they have passed, has now obtained a crisis throughout the place, so that there is scarcely a person to be found well enough to nurse those who are most afflicted by it.*[42]

Tucker expressed relief that his wife was not in Williamsburg to see what had occurred and declared that, "*As the British plundered all that they could, you*

---

[40] Tustin, ed., *Diary of the American War: A Hessian Journal*, 313.
[41] Stevens, ed., "The Southern Campaign, 1781: From Guildford Courthouse to the Siege of York: Narrated in the Letters from Judge St George Tucker to his Wife, July 11, 1781," *The Magazine of American History*, Vol. 7, 207-208.
[42] Ibid, 207.

will conceive how great an appearance of wretchedness this place must exhibit."[43]

General Cornwallis did not acknowledge any plundering, but did report to General Clinton in New York that his troops found a large supply of shot and shell in Williamsburg, which was seized for the use of his army.[44] According to Tucker, General Cornwallis also forced the inhabitants of Williamsburg to take paroles, pledging not to participate in the conflict until officially exchanged.[45]

At least one prominent resident of Williamsburg revealed his loyalist sympathies when Cornwallis and his army arrived. William Hunter, a printer and former co-publisher of the *Virginia Gazette* with John Dixon from 1775 through 1777, left Williamsburg with the British army in early July. General Cornwallis confirmed his service to the British army a year after the war ended.

> *Mr. William Hunter joined the army under my command at Williamsburgh in Virginia and rendered special service by procuring intelligence of the Enemy, & by every other means in his power; and that He afterwards bore arms at the siege of Yorktown in a Company of Volunteers.* [46]

---

[43] Ibid.

[44] Banastre Tarleton, "Earl Cornwallis to Sir Henry Clinton, June 30, 1781," *A History of the Campaigns of 1780 and 1781 in the Southern Provinces of North America*, (London: T. Cadell, in the Strand, 1787), 349.

[45] Stevens, ed., "The Southern Campaign, 1781: From Guildford Courthouse to the Siege of York: Narrated in the Letters from Judge St George Tucker to his Wife, July 11, 1781," *The Magazine of American History*, Vol. 7, 207-208.

[46] Mary A. Stephenson, *George Pitt House (LT) Historical Report, Block 18-2, Building 48*, Colonial Williamsburg Foundation Library Research Report Series, 1391, 1960, 43.

Hunter fled to New York, then Nova Scotia, and finally England, leaving his valuable property in Williamsburg behind.

The British army remained in Williamsburg for ten days and if General Cornwallis had had his way it would likely have been much longer. Orders from General Clinton in New York to send a portion of his army to New York caused Cornwallis to proceed to Portsmouth with his troops on July 4.

A week after their departure, St. George Tucker entered Williamsburg and commented to his wife that, "*Here* [the British] *remained for some days, and with them pestilence and famine took root, and poverty brought up the rear….*"[47]

Battle of Green Spring

In order to reach Portsmouth, General Cornwallis decided to ferry the army across the James River at Jamestown and then march from Surry County southward to Portsmouth. Before he crossed the river, however, Cornwallis tried to lure Lafayette into one last engagement. Sending Simcoe's Rangers across the river with the army's baggage on July 5, Cornwallis hid the rest of his troops along the northern shore. Pickets were placed on the road to Green Spring, a plantation two miles northeast of the river crossing. Cornwallis wanted to convince Lafayette that only the British rear guard remained on the north side of the river in hopes that the young French general would rashly attack. Cornwallis instructed his pickets to draw the Americans towards Jamestown and a trap.

Lafayette's advance guard, which numbered around five hundred troops under General Anthony Wayne, cautiously marched toward Jamestown in the early afternoon of July 6, and

---

[47] Stevens, ed., "The Southern Campaign, 1781: From Guildford Courthouse to the Siege of York: Narrated in the Letters from Judge St George Tucker to his Wife, July 11, 1781," *The Magazine of American History*, Vol. 7, 207-207.

halted at Green Spring at 2 p.m. Conflicting reports on the number of British troops that had crossed the river concerned Lafayette. He had no desire to risk his small army in a general engagement against Cornwallis. The young commander hoped instead for an opportunity to strike at the rearguard of the British as they crossed.

After an hour's pause at Green Spring, Lafayette, still uncertain of what enemy force lay to his front but determined to strike at Cornwallis in some way, ordered Wayne to advance his troops towards the ferry at Jamestown.

About half a mile into the march the road entered a long stretch of woods. Waiting in the woods were small parties of British skirmishers with orders to strongly resist the enemy advance, yet steadily fall back while doing so. An officer with the Seventy-Sixth Regiment recalled that the Americans,

> *First began by attacking a small picquet consisting of twenty Highlanders of the 76th, commanded by Lieut. Balyaird of the 80th, who being early wounded, Lieut. Alston of the same regiment…took the command of the picquet, he was also wounded. Lieut. Wemys…took command of the picquet. He had hardly had two minutes when he was wounded, and though half of the men were by this time killed or wounded the rest of the brave Highlanders kept their ground…till ordered in by Lord Cornwallis, but not before they expended about 50 rounds each man.*[48]

The British pickets—whose determined resistance and lack of reinforcement suggested to Wayne that his troops were

---

[48] *Caledonian Mercury*, October 10, 1781, "Extract of a letter from an officer in the 76th Regiment dated on board the *Lord Mulgrave* transport, Hampton Road, Virginia, July 23, 1781," 3.

indeed engaged with the rear guard of the British army—eventually withdrew from the woods. They hurried across an open field and redeployed among some out-buildings and fences of a farm.

Wayne's troops followed, marching straight at thousands of British troops hidden in the far wood line. Informed that a lone British cannon was struggling to withdraw near his right flank, Wayne ordered a detachment forward to seize it. That was the trigger for the British army to emerge from the woods and advance upon the Americans. Significantly outnumbered, General Wayne did the inconceivable, he ordered his troops to advance to meet the enemy. Lieutenant William Feltman of the First Pennsylvania Regiment described the advance:

> *Our advance* [was] *regular at a charge till we got within eighty yards of their whole army, they being regularly formed, standing one yard distance from each other... We advanced under a heavy fire of grape-shot at which distance we opened our musketry.*[49]

Ensign Ebenezer Denny of the same regiment recalled that, "*We could not have been engaged longer than about three or four minutes, but at a distance of sixty yards only.*"[50]

All who participated or witnessed the engagement noted the intensity of those few minutes of Wayne's advance. British lieutenant colonel Banastre Tarleton complimented the American troops for their gallantry:

---

[49] William Feltman, *Journal of Lt. William Feltman of the First Pennsylvania Regiment, 1781-1782*, (New York Times & Arno Press, 1969), 7.

[50] Ebenezer Denny, *Military Journal of Major Ebenezer Denny*, (Philadelphia: J.B. Lippincott and Co., 1859), 37.

> *The conflict in this quarter was severe and well contested. The artillery and infantry of each army…were for some minutes warmly engaged not fifty yards asunder…on the left of the British, the action was for some time gallantly maintained by the Continental infantry.*[51]

Wayne's advance against a vastly superior force came as a surprise to Cornwallis, who briefly halted his own advance. An American officer involved in the fight defended Wayne's action, noting that,

> *We could not possibly have extricated ourselves from the difficulties we were in but by the manouvre we adopted, which although it may have the appearance of temerity to those unacquainted with circumstances, yet was founded upon the truest military principles: And was one of those necessary, though daring measures, which seldom fail of producing the desired effect, that is, confusing the enemy and opening a way to retreat in sight of a much superior army.*[52]

General Wayne managed to extract the bulk of his army from Cornwallis's trap. The lateness of the day prevented the British from an aggressive pursuit, and with the armies disengaged, General Cornwallis proceeded to cross the river while General Wayne and Lafayette kept their distance.

Although the Battle of Green Spring was a British victory, American losses (which were approximately double the seventy

---

[51] Tarleton, *A History of the Campaigns of 1780 and 1781 in the Southern Provinces of North America*, 354.

[52] *Pennsylvania Packet*, "July 21, 1781, Extract of a letter from an officer of rank, July 11, 1781,"

men Cornwallis lost), could have been far worse.[53] In that sense, Green Spring was a missed opportunity for the British.

Summer Interlude

Two days after the battle, General Lafayette returned to the site of the Green Spring battle and the day after that he marched into Williamsburg. His stay there was brief, however, for he believed General Cornwallis was marching to the Carolina's to engage General Greene.[54] Lafayette intended to follow, and marched his army north to cross the James River.

Conflicting accounts of Cornwallis's intentions caused Lafayette to halt in Richmond, where he sent General Wayne's Pennsylvania continentals, with a regiment of newly raised Virginia continentals, across the James River to be in position to march south. He kept the remainder of his army near Richmond to wait and watch Cornwallis's actions.[55]

Weeks of inaction passed before the intentions of General Cornwallis became clear. In early August, the British evacuated Portsmouth and sailed to Yorktown. Compelled by General Clinton's orders to establish a secure base from which the British navy could harbor during the winter, Cornwallis chose Yorktown.

When General Washington in New York learned of this development as well as the intention of a powerful French fleet to sail to Chesapeake Bay for the autumn, he seized upon the opportunity to trap Cornwallis in Yorktown. Marching a

---

[53] Johnston, "Appendix 16: American Losses in the Action at Green Spring," *The Yorktown Campaign and the Surrender of Cornwallis, 1781,* 190.

[54] Idzerda, ed., "General LaFayette to Allen Jones, July 10, 1781," *LaFayette in the Age of the American Revolution: Selected Letters and Papers, 1776-1790*, Vol. 4, 241.

[55] Idzerda, ed., "General LaFayette to Anthony Wayne, July 15, 1781," *LaFayette in the Age of the American Revolution: Selected Letters and Papers, 1776-1790*, Vol. 4, 248-249.

portion of the American army along with the French army south to Virginia, Washington urged Lafayette to do all in his power to keep the British in Yorktown.[56]

Lafayette responded by marching southeastward from the outskirts of Richmond to New Kent County, where he could better observe British activity in and around Yorktown. General Wayne's troops also moved southeastward to be in position to block Cornwallis should he suddenly attempt to march south.

The success of the French navy against the British in the Battle of the Capes on September 5, severed Cornwallis's connection with the sea. It also allowed the American troops heading south from New York to be transported to Virginia by boat down the Chesapeake Bay. The noose was tightening around General Cornwallis in Yorktown, and Williamsburg would be the staging area for the pivotal clash to come.

---

[56] John C. Fitzpatrick, ed., "General Washington to General Lafayette, August 21, 1781," *The Writings of George Washington from the Original Manuscript Sources, 1745-1799*, Vol. 23, (U.S. Government Printing Office, 1937), 33-34.

Eight

Yorktown to the End
1781-1783

General Lafayette marched into Williamsburg with his troops on September 4, the day before the Battle of the Capes. Captain Benjamin Bartholomew, an officer with the Pennsylvania continentals, recorded in his diary that the troops were reviewed by both General Lafayette and General St. Simon, who had landed with over 3,000 French troops at Jamestown.[1] Bartholomew and his men were temporarily quartered in the college. He visited the city the next day and recorded his impressions in his diary.

> *This morning took a walk through the Town to view the public buildings, the College is on the West end of the Main Street (which is one Mile in length) it fronts the Capital which is on the East end, the College's front extends across the main street which is 110 feet broad; with two wings that extend in the rear fifty feet. The Capital's front extends across the main street...one hundred yards from the center of the Main Street on the North side is the Palace a large spacious building about fifty feet in front & one hundred & fifty deep, but at present is out of repair having been a*

---

[1] E. Lee Shepard, ed., "September 4, 1781," *Marching to Victory: Capt. Benjamin Bartholomew's Diary of the Yorktown Campaign, May 1781 to March 178*1, (Richmond: Virginia Historical Society, 2002), 21, and Idzerda, ed., "General LaFayette to the Chevalier de La Luzerne, September 8, 1781," *LaFayette in the Age of the American Revolution: Selected Letters and Papers, 1776-1790*, Vol. 4, 391.

> *hospital for some time. On the South Side of the main street is a hospital, where is a few Luniticks. The common buildings in this Town make no great appearance on the outside, but the Inside is elegant.*[2]

Lieutenant William Feltman, another continental officer from Pennsylvania, recorded his visit to Williamsburg in his journal that same day.

> *Took a walk to town with a number of our gentlemen, and took a view of the town, as it is the metropolis of Virginia. There are some very elegant buildings, such as the College, Palace, Capitol or State House.... As we passed through town Doct. Nicholson very politely asked us to walk with him to his house; we were very elegantly entertained with a good dinner, a glass of good spirits and Maderia wine.*[3]

General Lafayette's quarters in Williamsburg are difficult to locate with certainty, but Dr. Honyman offers a strong possibility in his journal. He recorded that Lafayette quartered at the college while in Williamsburg.[4]

On September 8, Lafayette informed the Chevalier de La Luzerne, who was still aboard a French naval ship, that nearly 6,000 French and American troops were in and around

---

[2] Shepard, ed., "September 5, 1781," *Marching to Victory: Capt. Benjamin Bartholomew's Diary of the Yorktown Campaign, May 1781 to March 178*1, 21.

[3] Feltman, "September 5, 1781," *The Journal of Lt. William Feltman, 1781-82*, 13.

[4] MacMaster, ed., "The Journal of Dr. Robert Honyman, April 17 – November 25, 1781," *Virginia Magazine of History and Biography*, 79, no. 4, 416.

Williamsburg.[5] Most were encamped on the outskirts of town. General Peter Muhlenberg commanded a thousand American troops posted about two miles east of Williamsburg on the road to Yorktown.[6] They included Pennsylvania and Virginia continentals who skirmished with British dragoons a day earlier.[7] Captain Bartholomew with the Pennsylvanians noted in his journal on September 8, that their stay on the picket line was short. They marched west four miles that day to, "*the rear of Williamsburgh to the grand Camp of ours &* [our] *allied army....*"[8] Virginia militia and riflemen took their place as advance pickets east of town, guarding the roads and passes from Yorktown to Williamsburg.[9]

The grand camp that Captain Bartholomew and his Pennsylvanians marched to was located about half a mile west of the Wren Building and just east of present day Matoaka Lake. The American camp was located on ground that is part of the campus of William and Mary. Some of the French troops also encamped on ground that is today part of the campus, but the

---

[5] Idzerda, ed., "General LaFayette to the Chevalier de La Luzerne, September 8, 1781," *LaFayette in the Age of the American Revolution: Selected Letters and Papers, 1776-1790*, Vol. 4, 391.

[6] Idzerda, ed., "General LaFayette to General Washington, September 8, 1781," *LaFayette in the Age of the American Revolution: Selected Letters and Papers, 1776-1790*, Vol. 4, 392.

Note: Today's Penniman Road follows much of the historic road trace all the way to Route 199.

[7] Shepard, ed., "September 7, 1781," *Marching to Victory: Capt. Benjamin Bartholomew's Diary of the Yorktown Campaign, May 1781 to March 1781*, 21.

[8] Shepard, ed., "September 8, 1781," *Marching to Victory: Capt. Benjamin Bartholomew's Diary of the Yorktown Campaign, May 1781 to March 1781*, 21.

[9] Edward M. Riley, ed., "St George Tucker's Journal of the Siege of Yorktown, 1781," *The William & Mary Quarterly*, Vol. 5, no. 3, (July, 1948), 377.

Note: This advance picket was located along today's Penniman Road.

bulk of the French encamped north of the road to Richmond (Route 60) in what is now a mixed residential and commercial neighborhood.[10]

It appears that Williamsburg was off limits to most of the troops. They spent an uneventful week waiting for Generals Washington and Rochambeau to arrive with reinforcements from the north. One pressing problem that weighed heavily on General Lafayette, however, was the shortage of provision, particularly flour, for the troops. He lamented to Governor Nelson on September 11, that, "*There is not one grain of flour in camp either for the American or French army. What we are to do I know not.*"[11] By the time Generals Washington and Rochambeau reached Williamsburg on September 14, the crisis had eased a bit, but remained a concern. Washington addressed the shortage in his general orders of the next day, declaring that,

> *He particularly admires the patience with which* [the French army] *supported the scarcity of Provisions that unfortunately existed at the time of their Junction owing to particular circumstances, circumstances which he exceedingly regrets, but hopes are already remedied and that the like misfortune will not be again experienced.*[12]

The arrival of the American and French commanders created a frenzy of excitement in Williamsburg. Lieutenant

---

[10] *Armee de Rochambeau, 1782, Carte des environs de Williamsburg en Virginia ou les armees froncoise et americaine ont camps en Septembre 1781*, Maps, Library of Congress.

[11] Idzerda, ed., "General LaFayette to Thomas Nelson, September 11, 1781," *LaFayette in the Age of the American Revolution: Selected Letters and Papers, 1776-1790*, Vol. 4, 398.

[12] Fitzpatrick, ed., "General Orders, September 15, 1781," *The Writings of George Washington*, Vol. 23, 114.

Feltman noted that, "*In the evening about four o' clock twenty-one pieces of cannon were fired on the arrival of his Excellency, General George Washington. There was a universal joy amongst our officers and soldiers, especially the French troops, on his arrival.*"[13] St. George Tucker provided a more detailed account of the reaction to their arrival.

> *About four o' clock in the afternoon his approach was announced. He had passed our camp, which is now in the rear of the whole army, before we had time to parade the militia. The French line had just time to form. The Continentals had more leisure. He approached without any pomp or parade, attended only by a few horsemen and his own servants. The Count de Rochambeau and General* [Edward] *Hand, with one or two more officers were with him. I met him as I was endeavoring to get to camp from town, in order to parade the brigade; but he had already passed it. To my great surprise he recognized my features and spoke to me immediately after. General Nelson, the Marquis, etc., rode up immediately after. Never was more joy painted in any countenance than theirs. The Marquis rode up with precipitation, clasped the General in his arms, and embraced him with an ardor not easily described. The whole army and all the town were presently in motion. The General, at the request of the Marquis de St. Simon, rode through the French lines. The troops paraded for the purpose and cut a most splendid figure. He then visited the Continental line. As he entered the camp*

---

[13] Feltman, "September 14, 1781," *The Journal of Lt. William Feltman, 1781-82*, 13.

> *the cannon from the Park of Artillery and from every brigade announced the happy event. His train by this time was much increased; and men, women and children seemed to via with each other in demonstrations of joy and eagerness to see their beloved countryman. His quarters are at Mr. Wythe's house. Aunt Betty* [Elizabeth Randolph] *has the honor of the Count de Rochambeau to lodge at her house. We are all alive and so sanguine in our hopes that nothing can be conceived more different than the countenances of the same men at this time and on the first of June. The troops which were to attend the General are coming down the bay.... Cornwallis may now tremble for his fate, for nothing but some extraordinary interposition of his guardian angels seems capable of saving him and the whole army from captivity.*[14]

Ensign Ebenezer Denny with the Pennsylvania continentals also described the effect the arrival of General Washington and his staff had on the army. "*The presence of so many general officers, and the arrival of new corps, seem to give additional life to everything. Discipline the order of the day. In all directions troops seen exercising and maneuvering.*"[15]

This did not hold true of course for the troops posted east of town on the picket line. Colonel Tucker recalled in his diary that, "*General Muhlenberg in the meantime had made frequent*

---

[14] Lyon G. Tyler, "Col. St. George Tucker to his Wife, September 15, 1781," *Williamsburg, the Old Capital*, (Richmond, VA: Whittet & Shepperson, 1907), 83-84.

[15] Denny, "September 15, 1781," *Military Journal of Major Ebenezer Denny*, 39.

excursions to the Lines of the British near York, but nothing material happened as he could not draw the Enemy out on any Occasion."[16]

General Washington had a number of issues to address upon his arrival, but the shortage of provision for the troops remained the most pressing. Within a day of his arrival, he wrote to Congress, the governor of Maryland, the Board of War, and several American officers seeking means to alleviate the shortage. He ordered his Quarter Master to appropriate a sufficient number of nearby cornfields to feed his troops, but insisted that it be done in an orderly way, forbidding the soldiers from taking corn from any field except those, "*pointed out by the Quarter Master.*"[17]

For those few soldiers able to leave camp, (typically officers) such as Lieutenant Feltman and Captain Bartholomew, crabs and oysters from College and Queen's Creek were too tempting to resist. Feltman noted in his journal on September 17, that, "*This morning went to College Landing, crabbing; we caught three dozen. We also had a great deal of diversion in catching them.*"[18]

The first of the American and French troops from New York arrived at Burwell's Landing on September 22.[19] They continued to arrive over the next four days, some landing at

---

[16] Riley, ed., "St George Tucker's Journal of the Siege of Yorktown, 1781," *The William & Mary Quarterly*, Vol. 5, no. 3, 379.
[17] Fitzpatrick, ed., "General Orders, September 16, 1781," *The Writings of George Washington,* Vol. 23, 122.
[18] Feltman, "September 17, 1781," *The Journal of Lt. William Feltman, 1781-82*, 14, and Shepard, ed., "September 20, 1778," *Marching to Victory: Capt. Benjamin Bartholomew's Diary of the Yorktown Campaign, May 1781 to March 178*1, 22.
[19] Feltman, "September 22, 1781," *The Journal of Lt. William Feltman, 1781-82*, 14, and Shepard, ed., "September 22, 1778," *Marching to Victory: Capt. Benjamin Bartholomew's Diary of the Yorktown Campaign, May 1781 to March 178*1, 22.

Burwell's, others College Landing, and still others at Jamestown. They then marched into Williamsburg and encamped near the capitol on the east end of town.[20] Jean-Francois-Louis, Comte de Clermont-Crevecoeur an artillery officer and French nobleman, recorded his impression of Williamsburg in his journal.

> *Williamsburg is situated on a charming plain between two creeks that flow into the James and York rivers. The town itself is not particularly pretty and consists of a single very long street at either end of which are very handsome buildings.... The streets are not paved and are very rough in both summer and winter.*[21]

On September 27, General Washington repositioned the troops encamped west of Williamsburg; they marched through town and joined the newly arrived northern troops camped near the capitol. Rations of bread or flour and meat for four days were issued to all the American troops. The march to Yorktown would commence the next day at 5 a.m.[22] To protect the supply magazines established in Williamsburg as well as the city itself, Washington left nearly eight hundred troops behind. He explained to Admiral de Grasse, the French naval commander, that he could ill afford to lose the men for the siege, "*but unless this detachment is made, the Enemy might in the greatest*

---

[20] Shepard, ed., "September 25, 1781," *Marching to Victory: Capt. Benjamin Bartholomew's Diary of the Yorktown Campaign, May 1781 to March 178*1, 22.

[21] Howard C. Rice and Anne S.K. Brown, trans. and eds., "Clermont-Crevecoeur Journal, September 26, 1781," *The American Campaigns of Rochambeau's Army, 1780*-83, Vol. 1, (Princeton, NJ and Providence, RI: Princeton University Press, Brown University Press, 1972), 56.

[22] Fitzpatrick, ed., "General Orders, September 27, 1781," *The Writings of George Washington,* Vol. 23, 146-148.

security land above Queen's Creek to cover his left flank, and by a very short march effect the most destructive purposes...."[23]

Siege of Yorktown

When the allied army began its march at dawn on September 28, thousands of American continentals, Virginia militia, and French soldiers proceeded along the same route, the Yorktown Road. Much of this route is still accessible today as a modern road, the Penniman Road in York County.[24]

There were only two possible land approaches to Yorktown for the allies. A narrow approach existed along the shoreline of the York River to the west of town, and a much broader approach extended from the southeast side of the town to the river on the east side of town. The York River covered any approach to the town from the north and between the two land approaches was a wide, impassable, morass, west of the town.

About four miles from Yorktown the allied army split. The French followed a road that took them towards the York River while the Americans veered right and followed a route that placed them south of the town. Only a portion of the French army encamped near the western shoreline approach to Yorktown, it was defended by a strong British fort or redoubt. The bulk of the French army was posted to the left of the American army on the southern approach to Yorktown. Both armies were over a mile from the British works when they halted for the night; the troops slept under the stars on their arms as a precaution.[25]

---

[23] Fitzpatrick, ed., "General Washington to Comte De Grasse, October 1, 1781," *The Writings of George Washington*, Vol. 23, 160.

[24] *Armee de Rochambeau, 1782, Carte des environs de Williamsburg en Virginia ou les armees froncoise et americaine ont camps en Septembre 1781*, Maps, Library of Congress.

[25] Jerome A. Greene, *The Guns of Independence: The Siege of Yorktown, 1781,* (El Dorado Hills, CA: Savas Beatie, 2005), 95.

The next day, General Washington extended the American position to the York River and the following day the allies were thrilled to discover that General Cornwallis had abandoned most of his outer works. Assured by General Clinton that relief from New York was on its way, Cornwallis opted not to sacrifice his men in the exposed outworks.[26] He maintained just three, the Fusiliers Redoubt on the riverbank west of town, and Redoubts 9 and 10 on the riverbank east of town.

Cornwallis's action sped up the allied timetable. The abandoned positions were occupied and the first siege line was dug on the evening of October 6, approximately six hundred yards from the British works. Colonel Richard Butler with the Pennsylvania continentals described the process:

> *The first parallel and other works being laid out by the engineer; a body of troops* [were] *ordered...to break ground and form works, the materials being got ready and brought previously to the spot.*[27]

Sergeant Joseph Plum Martin of Connecticut recalled that General Washington himself ceremoniously started the American trench with a pick ax:

> *The troops of the line were there ready with entrenching tools and began to entrench, after General Washington had struck a few blows with a pickax, a mere ceremony.... The ground was sandy*

[26] William B. Wilcox, ed., "Extract of minutes of a council of war held at New York, September 24, 1781," *The American Rebellion: Sir Henry Clinton's Narrative of His Campaign*, (New Haven: Yale University Press, 1954), 574.
[27] Henry S. Commager and Richard B. Morris, "Journal of Colonel Richard Butler, October 6, 1781," *The Spirit of Seventy-Six*, (Edison, NJ: Castle Books, 2002), 1229.

> *and soft, and the men employed that night* [were not idle], *so that by daylight they had covered themselves from danger from the enemy's shot.*[28]

Surgeon James Thacher observed the opening of the parallel and recalled:

> *This business was conducted with great silence and secrecy, and we were favored by Providence with a night of extreme darkness, and were not discovered before day-light. The working party carried on their shoulder fascines and intrenching tools, while a large part of the detachment was armed with the implements of death. Horses, drawing cannon and ordnance, and wagons loaded with bags filled with sand for constructing breastworks, flowed in the rear.*[29]

The British discovered the new allied works at sunrise and unleashed an intense artillery barrage. Over the course of the next two days, American and French work parties labored to improve the fortifications and construct battery positions for their cannon, all under a steady, but ineffective, British bombardment.

The allies completed construction of their first artillery batteries on October 9, and responded to the British bombardment with one of their own. General Washington reportedly commenced the American bombardment, touching off an eighteen pound cannon whose solid shot smashed through a building with British officers inside, killing one

---

[28] Joseph Plum Martin, *Private Yankee Doolittle*, (Harrisonburg, PA: Eastern Acorn Press, 1962), 232.

[29] James Thacher, *Military Journal of the American Revolution*, (Gansevoort, NY: Corner House Historical Publications, 1998),281-282.

instantly and tearing the leg off another.[30] Captain James Duncan of Pennsylvania, recalled that,

> *The whole night was nothing but one continual roar of cannon, mixed with the bursting of shells and rumbling of houses torn to pieces. As soon as the day approached the enemy withdrew their pieces from their embrazures and retired under cover of their works, and now commenced a still more dreadful cannonade from all our batteries without scarcely any intermission for the whole day.*[31]

Captain Johann Ewald with the British army described the allied bombardment from inside the British earthworks.

> *Since yesterday the besiegers have fired bombshells incessantly.... The great part of the town lies in ashes, and two* [or our] *batteries have already been completely dismantled.*[32]

The heavy allied bombardment continued day and night. Lieutenant Bartholomew James, a British naval officer detached from his ship to serve on an artillery battery in the British works described the suffering those trapped in Yorktown, soldier and civilian alike, experienced.

> *Upwards of a thousand shells were thrown into the works on this night* [October 11] *and every spot*

---

[30] Greene, *The Guns of Independence: The Siege of Yorktown, 1781,* 191.
[31] William H. Egle, ed., "Diary of Captain James Duncan of Colonel Moses Hazen's Regiment in the Yorktown Campaign, 1781," *Pennsylvania Archives, 2nd Series*, Vol. 15, (1890), 751.
[32] Tustin, ed., *Diary of the American War: A Hessian Journal*, 334.

> *became alike dangerous. The noise and thundering of the cannon, the distressing cries of the wounded, and the lamentable sufferings of the inhabitants, whose dwellings were chiefly in flames, added to the restless fatigues of the duty, must inevitably fill every mind with pity and compassion who are possessed of any feelings for their fellow creatures.*[33]

The heavy allied cannon fire provided cover for the troops charged with digging a second parallel on October 11. Lieutenant Feltman was with the troops who dug the new trench just three hundred yards from the enemy works. He described the effort in his journal.

> *Just at dusk we advanced within gun-shot of the enemy, then began our work. In one hour's time we had ourselves completely covered, so we disregarded their cannonading; they discharged a number of pieces at our party, but they had but little effect and only wounded one of our men. We were in the center of two fires, from the enemy and our own....*[34]

The British increased their own bombardment upon the allied troops in the second parallel. A French officer noted that,

> *The day was spent in cannonading and firing bombs at each other in such profusion that we did one another much damage. The enemy seemed to have been saving up their ammunition for the second parallel. It was of*

---

[33] John K. Laughton, ed., *The Journal of Rear-Admiral Bartholomew James*, (1896), 122.

[34] Feltman, "September 22, 1781," *The Journal of Lt. William Feltman, 1781-82*, 19. 19.

very small caliber and very effective, being fired at short range. That night we had six men killed and twenty-eight wounded.[35]

While the French and Americans suffered casualties, they were just a fragment of the losses General Cornwallis suffered. Lieutenant James of the British navy described the carnage his men suffered in the British hornwork, a fortified position of the British earthwork less than two hundred yards from the French batteries.

In fifty-two minutes after my arrival in the hornwork the enemy silenced the three guns left by closing the embrasures, shortly after which they dismounted a twelve pounder, knocked off the muzzles of two eighteens, and for the last hour and a half left me with one eighteen-pounder with a part of its muzzle also shot away, which I kept up a fire till it was also rendered useless.[36]

As he neared the end of his eight hour shift in the hornwork, James was nearly killed by a shell that burst nearby, giving him a contusion on his face and leg. He recounted in his journal that his detachment was utterly destroyed in the hornwork:

During my stay in the works [I] *had nine men killed, twenty-seven wounded, eight of which died* [since] *they were removed and most of the wounded had lost on arm or leg, and some both. In short, myself and the midshipman, both wounded were the only two*

---

[35] Rice and Brown, eds., "Clermont-Crevecoeur Journal," *The American Campaigns of Rochambeau's Army*, Vol. 1, 59.
[36] Laughton, ed., *The Journal of Rear-Admiral Bartholomew James*, 124.

> *returned out of thirty-six, having stood a close cannonade with the enemy for eight hours, who had ninety-seven pieces of heavy cannon playing on us all that time.*[37]

Dr. James Thacher provided a vivid description from the American lines of the constant shelling between the two sides.

> *Being in the trenches every other night and day, I have a fine opportunity of witnessing the sublime and stupendous scene which is continually exhibiting. The bomb-shells from the besiegers and the besieged are incessantly crossing each other's path in the air. They are clearly visible in the form of a black ball in the day, but in the night, they appear like a fiery meteor with a blazing tail, most beautifully brilliant, ascending majestically form the mortar to a certain altitude, and gradually descending to the spot they are destined to execute their work of destruction.... When a shell falls, it whirls round, burrows and excavates the earth to a considerable extent, and bursting, makes a dreadful havoc around. I have more than once witnessed fragments of the mangled bodies and limbs of the British soldiers thrown into the air by the bursting of our shells....*[38]

Two British redoubts in front of the main British earthworks prevented the Americans from completing their second parallel to the York River. On the evening of October 14, two allied detachments, one American and the other French,

---

[37] Ibid.
[38] Thacher, *Military Journal of the American Revolution*, 284.

successfully stormed the redoubts. The following evening the British sent a sortie from their lines to attack a portion of the allied second parallel, but the raid caused minimal damage and did little to slow the allied bombardment. On the evening of October 16, General Cornwallis attempted to evacuate his army across the York River in a desperate attempt to escape, but a sudden thunderstorm scattered his boats and ended the effort. The next day Cornwallis asked for terms of surrender and two days after that the British army surrendered at Yorktown.

For ten months Williamsburg, and much of Virginia, had lived on edge, concerned that British troops under General Arnold, or Phillips, or Cornwallis would descend upon their city at any moment and destroy it. On October 21, many of Williamsburg's inhabitants watched with great satisfaction as the very soldiers they dreaded marched through their city as prisoners, guarded by the same militia that was powerless to stop them the previous winter, spring, or summer. [39] Although the entire British army did not march through Williamsburg that day, thousands of Cornwallis's troops did. The British troops captured across the York River in Gloucester marched to Fredericksburg and both detachments ended up in Winchester, in northwest Virginia.

One of the German soldiers who marched with Cornwallis's army to Winchester recorded his observations of Williamsburg in a journal. He noted that,

> *The city consists of approximately 300 houses, and is fairly built up for a mile in length. It is secured by strong forts and good earthworks.... The city lies upon*

---

[39] Riley, ed., "St George Tucker's Journal of the Siege of Yorktown, 1781," *The William & Mary Quarterly*, Vol. 5, no. 3, 394.

> *an agreeable open plain. While it is not, it is true, so very large, one may nevertheless count it among the beautiful cities of America. From the distinction of formerly having been the capital city of Virginia and the seat of government, now only the title remains. It has some beautiful churches and steeples with clocks to see, and also some buildings otherwise worth seeing.... There is also a beautiful, large state house, where the General Court assembles, out of which a Latin school should be established in the future. At the local University there are at present 7 professors and 50 students.... Here also were many French and American hospitals, where they had brought all their sick and wounded. Also there was still in the city a strong garrison of about 1,000 French and Americans.*[40]

The inhabitants of Williamsburg played an important role in support of the allied siege of Yorktown. Many supplied the allied army with food, forage, livestock, and accommodations before and during the siege. Washington assured one prominent resident of the city, Elizabeth Randolph, whose home General Rochambeau had stayed in during his time in Williamsburg, that, "*measures* [are adopting] *for making an equitable compensation to the Inhabitants for such Articles as have been taken for the use of the Allied Army*."[41] In other words, payment for food, forage, livestock, etc., impressed by the allied army during its stay in Virginia, would be forthcoming.

---

[40] Carson, ed., "The Doehla Journal, October 22, 1781," *We Were There: Descriptions of Williamsburg, 1699-1859*, 55.

[41] Fitzpatrick, ed., "General Washington to Betty Randolph, October 25, 1781," *The Writings of George Washington*, Vol. 23, 265-266.

The governor's palace and one of the college buildings were used as hospitals for the sick and wounded troops and several important supply magazines were maintained in the city. By the end of the siege approximately four hundred sick and wounded men were quartered in the hospitals.[42] Dr. James Craik, who oversaw their care, expressed his concern to Washington about the severe shortage of supplies needed for them.

> *We have a number in the small pox and they are daily increasing, more house room will be wanted in Williamsburg when the army moves. All the Hospitals are destitute of Blankets, shirts, overalls and cloathing all essentially necessary for the recovery of the sick. The Department is entirely destitute of money, there is not nor has there been a single copper to pay a nurse or an orderly or to purchase milk or vegetables; and in a short time stores and medicine will be wanting. I have taken every method to have them sent on from Philadelphia by writing the purveyor repeatedly but have not received any answer to my letters, nor any stores or medicines. The sick I am afraid will suffer if their dependence is to be from that quarter, and more certainly so if the fleet should leave the Bay. . . Sugar and coffee will not be wanted for some time, Rice and wine are now wanted. The putrid diseases that now prevail in the Hospital and the wounded require wine, as it is the best cordial that can be given them.*[43]

---

[42] Herbert S. Ragland, Department of Research, "Dr. James Craig to General Washington, October 23, 1781," *The Governor's Palace: Historical Notes*," Colonial Williamsburg Foundation Library Research Report Series, 219, 1930, 279.
[43] Ibid.

General Washington replied to Dr. Craik that same day. He did not offer a solution to the shortages that plagued the hospitals, but he did stress that,

> *As many of the Sick as can be provided for must be accommodated in Williamsburg; if additional Houses are wanted for that purpose, the Quarter Master Genl. must provide them, and likewise a separate House either in or near that place for the reception of your Small pox patients....*[44]

Reverend James Madison and the professors of William and Mary were eager to restore some normalcy to the college after all the turmoil of the past year and wrote to General Washington at the conclusion of the siege to request that the sick and wounded soldiers quartered in the president's residence be moved someplace else. Washington assured them that they would indeed be moved, "*as soon as Circumstances will permit.*" [45] The opportunity never arrived; the residence was damaged by fire on November 24. General Rochambeau informed General Washington that, "*we carried away all the sick, and all the furniture, but could only think about hindering the communication of the fire with the main building.*"[46]

---

[44] Fitzpatrick, ed., "General Washington to Dr. Craik, October 23, 1781," *The Writings of George Washington*, Vol. 23, 256-257.

[45] Fitzpatrick, ed., "General Washington to the President and Professors of the University of William and Mary, October 27, 1781," *The Writings of George Washington*, Vol. 23, 276-277.

[46] W.A.R. Goodwin, "General Rochambeau to General Washington, December 24, 1781," *House History File, George Wythe House Historical Report*: Colonial Williamsburg Foundation Library Research Report Series 1484, 1938, 16-17.

The Governor's Palace also continued to serve as a hospital into the winter, but it was ill suited because three large rooms did not have fireplaces and the iron stoves that had heated the rooms in the past had been removed when the capital moved to Richmond. Timothy Pickering, the Quarter Master General of the American Army, wrote to Governor Nelson on November 8, in search of the missing stoves. Pickering explained that,

> *There are three large rooms at the palace destitute of fire places: and the sick cannot remain in them unless stoves can be procured. Mr. Holt thinks those* [stoves] *formerly belonging to the palace were removed to Richmond. As I know not where to procure any, and these rooms are essential for our sick, I request your excellency will be so kind as to cause the palace stoves to be sent hither as quick as possible, as the sick have already suffered by the cold.*[47]

With the British threat to Virginia eliminated, most Virginians desired to move on with their lives. This concerned General Washington, who worried that the victory at Yorktown might make Virginians, if not all Americans, overconfident and more complaisant about the war. He expressed his concern to Governor Nelson a week after the surrender.

> *I will candidly confess to Your Excellency, that my only apprehension (which I wish may be groundless), is, lest the late important success, instead of exciting our exertions, as it ought to do, should produce such a*

---

[47] Department of Research, "Timothy Pickering, Q.M.G. to Governor Nelson, November 8, 1781," *The Governor's Palace: Historical Notes*," Colonial Williamsburg Foundation Library Research Report Series, 219, 1930, 282.

relaxation in the prosecution of the War, as will prolong the calamities of it.[48]

Washington intended to keep pressure on the British by sending the Pennsylvania, Maryland and Virginia continentals at Yorktown to General Greene in South Carolina. The rest of the continental army would return to New York with Washington to maintain pressure on the British there. The French navy was eager to return to the Caribbean to protect French possessions there, but General Rochambeau decided to remain in Virginia with his troops, garrisoned in Williamsburg, Yorktown, Hampton, and West Point for the winter.[49] No doubt the harsh winter of the previous year influenced his decision.

General Washington and the American army left Yorktown on November 5. Although they likely passed through Williamsburg on his way north, General Washington did not stop, for on November 6, he was with his wife in New Kent County, comforting her at the loss of her last child, John Parke Custis. Washington's step son had served as an aide at Yorktown but contracted camp fever.[50] His death was a very bitter ending to the Yorktown campaign for the Washingtons.

The French in Williamsburg

With the departure of the American army and French navy and the dismissal of the militia, all that remained of the allied presence in Yorktown was General Rochambeau's French

---

48 Fitzpatrick, ed., "General Washington to Governor Thomas Nelson, October 27, 1781," *The Writings of George Washington*, Vol. 23, 271.

49 Fitzpatrick, ed., "General Washington to General Nathanael Greene, October 31, 1781," *The Writings of George Washington*, Vol. 23, 311.

50 Fitzpatrick, ed., "General Washington to the President of Congress, November 6, 1781," and "General Washington to the Marquis de Lafayette, November 15, 1781," *The Writings of George Washington*, Vol. 23, 338, 340.

army. He left one regiment in Yorktown, posted another in Hampton, ordered a detachment of artillery to the small town of West Point at the head of the York River, and ordered the remaining two French regiments, with several companies of artillery, to Williamsburg.[51] Rochambeau and his staff took up residence at George Wythe's home, General Washington's former headquarters.[52]

To at least one French officer who recorded his experience in Williamsburg, the city's inhabitants were thrilled by the presence of the French.

> *One could not be more hospitable than are the inhabitants of Williamsburg to all the army officers; they receive them very cordially in their homes and do all in their power to provide entertainment for them.... In this city, the fair sex, although they are not the prettiest I have seen, form a very agreeable and, in general, very well bred society.*[53]

It is not difficult to understand why Williamsburg's residents embraced the French army in their city. The departure of the state government to Richmond eighteen months earlier, the city's economic engine, was a severe blow to Williamsburg's merchants and inhabitants. Months of

---

[51] Rice and Brown, trans. and eds., "Journal of Jean-Baptiste-Antoine de Verger," *The American Campaigns of Rochambeau's Army, 1780*-83, Vol. 1, 152.

[52] Goodwin, "General Rochambeau to General Washington, December 24, 1781," *House History File, George Wythe House Historical Report*: Colonial Williamsburg Foundation Library Research Report Series 1484, 1938, 16-17.

[53] Carson, ed., "Diary Entry of Baron von Closen, November 24, 1781," *We Were There: Descriptions of Williamsburg, 1699-1859*, 50.

disruption caused by two British occupations and the constant threat of another attack brought economic hardship in 1781.

The arrival of the American and French armies in the fall offered some relief to the commerce starved city; the needs of thousands of troops and hundreds of draft animals had to be met. Although the paper currency offered by the Americans was nearly worthless, the French offered hard specie (coin) for payment. Their arrival and continued stay in Williamsburg was thus an economic blessing to many of the city's inhabitants.

Based on the journals of several French officers, they were fascinated with both the natural wonders of Virginia as well as the character and custom of the people. One officer posted at West Point over the winter recorded candid observations of Virginians that likely applied to those in Williamsburg as well.

> *These people are very hospitable and receive you in a most cordial manner, but they are exceptionally lazy. The gentlemen, as well as those who claim to be but are not, live like lords. Like all Americans they are generally cold, but the women are warmer. They have the advantage of being much gayer by nature than the northern women, though not so pretty. They love pleasure and are passionately fond of dancing, in which they indulge in both summer and winter. When a gentleman goes out of his house – something he does rarely – he is always followed by a negro groom who rides behind him.*[54]

Detailed description of Virginia's wildlife, plants, terrain, and climate, appear in many of the French journals. One officer

---

[54] Rice and Brown, trans. and eds., "Clermont-Crevecoeur Journal," *The American Campaigns of Rochambeau's Army*, Vol. 1, 66.

noted that General Rochambeau, like General Washington, thoroughly enjoyed fox hunts and went several times a week whenever conditions allowed.[55] One can imagine that, given the propensity of Virginians to dance and entertain, General Rochambeau and his officers also found plenty of opportunity to enjoy one of the favorite activities of Virginians.

Although both the French and their hosts in Williamsburg seemed satisfied with their stay in the city, their presence in Williamsburg was not incident free. On November 23, Reverend Madison's residence, which was used as a hospital for French soldiers, was damaged by fire. Rochambeau conveyed the news to General Washington in late December following yet another fire that destroyed the governor's palace.

> *The Wing of the College where we Lodged our wounded officers had begun to be burnt down, we carried away all the sick, and all the furniture, but could only think about hindering the communication of the fire with the main building. Last night, the same accident happened to the Palace, in which was the American hospital, all the sick were saved as well as the greatest part of the effects, and we hindered the fire from communicating to the neighbouring houses, to mine* [the Wythe House] *especially; it is the one occupied by your Excellency, it was covered all the night long with a rain of red hot ashes. We have put all your sick in the Capitol, and today have had all which was possible for us to furnish them with* [delivered to them]. *At Colonel Menzies's requisition I have ordered a guard to be set around it to prevent the*

---

[55] Rice and Brown, trans. and eds., "Journal of Jean-Baptiste-Antoine de Verger," *The American Campaigns of Rochambeau's Army, 1780*-83, Vol. 1, 158.

> *same accident, and I have caused the precaution to be tripled* [at] *our hospital at the College...*[56]

General Rochambeau agreed to pay $12,000 pounds for the damage caused to the college building as well as the loss of a significant part of Reverend Madison's library and several pieces of physics equipment.[57] There was no French compensation for the governor's palace, which lay in ruins for years after the fire. That was the responsibility of the American government.

The French remained in Williamsburg and the surrounding area through June 1782. Unaccustomed to Virginia's summer, many suffered through the heat and humidity. An officer posted in West Point observed in his journal that,

> *We suffered greatly from the heat. The nights seemed even hotter than the days. We did not know where to turn. Added to this discomfort was an invasion of gnats, whose bite is far more venomous than those of Europe.... During the summer it is impossible to go out of the house in the daytime. The houses are designed to stay cool, being built round a large hall or vestibule with a cross draft running through it. This serves as a sitting room during the day. In the evening you go out, but you do not stay long outdoors since the dampness of the night air is dangerous. The*

---

[56] Goodwin, "General Rochambeau to General Washington, December 24, 1781," *House History File, George Wythe House Historical Report*: Colonial Williamsburg Foundation Library Research Report Series 1484, 1938, 16-17.

[57] Carson, ed., "Diary Entry of Baron von Closen, November 24, 1781," *We Were There: Descriptions of Williamsburg, 1699-1859*, 50.

> *Americans stand the heat better than we do, or at least they are less sensitive to it.*[58]

When orders to march back to New York were issued in late June, they no doubt came as a relief to many of the French soldiers who wished to avoid the rest of Virginia's searing summer. The bulk of the French army marched north on July 1st. Their departure ushered in a new era for Williamsburg, one of a sleepy Virginia town.

The Revolutionary War did not officially end until 1783 when the conflicting sides signed the Treaty of Paris. For the inhabitants of Williamsburg, however, the war ended when General Rochambeau's French troops marched away in the summer of 1782. They left behind a city that lost a quarter of its population over the course of the war, declining from 1,900 residents in 1775 to just over 1,400 in 1782. A 1782 census of the city's population counted 722 white residents and 702 black residents, eleven of who were free.[59]

The state government's move to Richmond in 1780 was the chief cause of the city's decline; many of the taverns and trades that catered to government officials and those who visited the city on government business shut down, some moving to Richmond and others just closed. The presence of the French army in 1782 delayed the economic decline momentary, but it resumed with the departure of the French. Just six months after the French marched away, Reverend Francis Asbury visited Williamsburg and noted in his journal that,

---

[58] Rice and Brown, trans. and eds., "Clermont-Crevecoeur Journal," *The American Campaigns of Rochambeau's Army*, Vol. 1, 71.

[59] Michael Nicholls, *Aspects of the African American Experience in Eighteenth Century Williamsburg and Norfolk*, Colonial Williamsburg Foundation Library Research Report Series, 330, 1990, 9-10.

> *The place has suffered and is suffering; the palace, the barracks, and some good dwelling -houses burnt. The capitol is no great building, and is going to ruin; the exterior of the college not splendid, and but few students.*[60]

Alexander Macaulay visited Williamsburg with his wife in February 1783 and was informed that there was but one public house (tavern) still open in the city.[61] Dr. Johann David Schoepf also visited Williamsburg in 1783 and provided a bleak description of the city.

> *Williamsburg is now a poor place compared with its former splendor. With the removal of the government, merchants, advocates, and other considerable residents took their departure as well, and the town has lost half its population. The trade of this place was never great, its distance from navigable waters not being favorable to more active affairs.... The inhabitants of this town and of all lower Virginia desire greatly that the seat of government should be brought back thither.*[62]

Alas, the state capital did not return to Williamsburg and remains to this day in Richmond. Williamsburg, the city that played such a crucial role in the American Revolution and

---

[60] Carson, ed., "Journal of Rev. Francis Ashbury, December 11, 1782," *We Were There: Descriptions of Williamsburg, 1699-1859*, 67.

[61] Carson, ed., "Journal of Alexander Macauley," *We Were There: Descriptions of Williamsburg, 1699-1859*, 70.

[62] Carson, ed., "Travels in the Confederation from the German of Johann David Schoepf," *We Were There: Descriptions of Williamsburg, 1699-1859*, 73-74.

Revolutionary War, became one of the conflict's victims, replaced and forgotten.

Of course, the fact that Williamsburg saw little growth or development in the century and a half following the Revolution is one of the key reasons behind its successful restoration today. To date, eighty-nine original building have been restored and many more, including the Governor's Palace, Capitol, and Raleigh Tavern, have been rebuilt. None of this would have likely occurred had Williamsburg remained Virginia's capital. The city's colonial past would have long ago been swallowed up by development.

So, in an ironic way, the same Revolutionary War that doomed Williamsburg to obscurity and decline planted the seeds for its future rejuvenation and development as one of the premier colonial historic sites in the United States. Today, visitors can travel to Williamsburg and walk in the footsteps of those who led, fought, and struggled for American independence. They can visit the very ground and often the very buildings that played such an important role in the American Revolution. And they can travel back in time, however briefly, to better appreciate the pivotal role Williamsburg played in the American Revolution and the Revolutionary War.

Map of Southeast Virginia

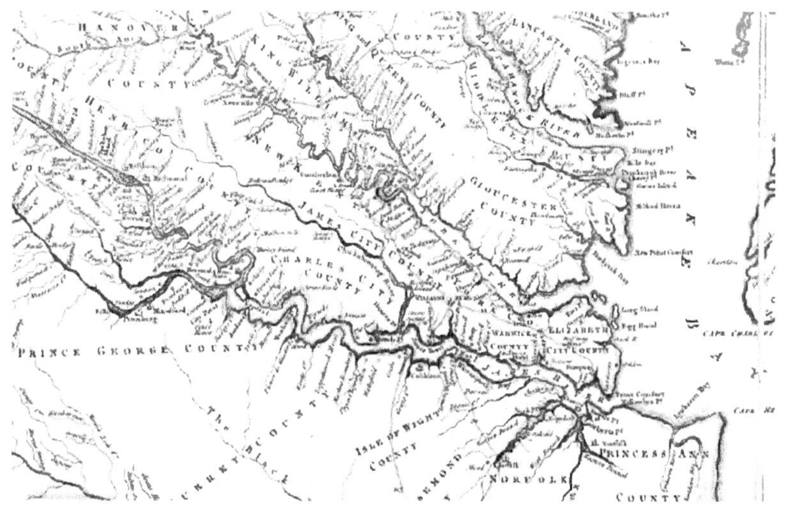

Map of Williamsburg & Vicinity : 1781

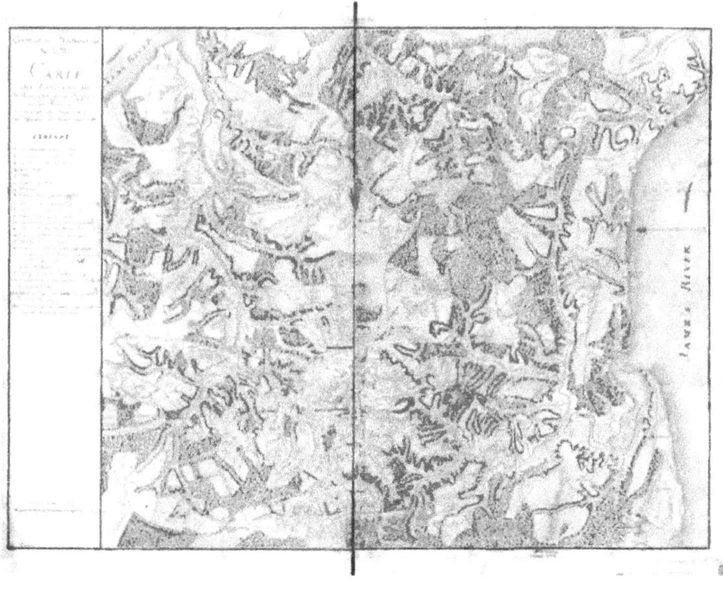

Frenchman's Map of Williamsburg : 1782

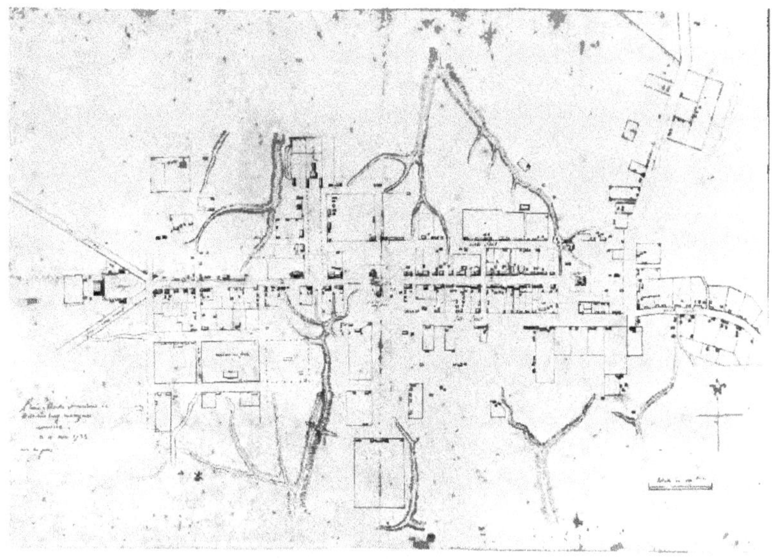

Source: Frenchman's Map, Special Collections Research Center, William & Mary Libraries

Capitol Building

Governor's Palace

Bruton Church

Wren Building : College of William and Mary

President's Residence : College of William and Mary

George Wythe Residence

Peyton Randolph Residence

Powder Magazine

Courthouse

Gaol

Raleigh Tavern

Duke of Gloucester Street

Bibliography

Primary Sources

Journal of a French Traveler in the Colonies, [New York 1921] Pdf.https//www.loc.gov/item/ca33000046/.

Abbott, W.W., et al. *The Papers of George Washington.* Charlottesville, VA: University Press of Virginia, 1987-.

Annual Register for the Year 1776, 4th ed.

Boyd, Julian P., ed. *The Papers of Thomas Jefferson.* Vol. 2-5. Princeton, NJ: Princeton University Press, 1950-1952.

Brock, R. A., ed. "Papers, Military and Political, 1775-1778 of George Gilmer, M.D. of Pen Park, Albemarle Co., VA," *Miscellaneous Papers 1672-1865 Now First Printed from the Manuscripts in the Virginia Historical Society.* Richmond, VA, 1937.

Campbell, Charles, ed. *The Bland Papers: Being a Selection from the Manuscript of Colonel Theodorick Bland Jr.* Vol. 1. 1840.

Campbell, Charles, ed., *The Orderly Book of that Portion of the American Army Stationed at or near Williamsburg, Virginia under the Command of General Andrew Lewis, from March 18, 1776 to August 28, 1776*. Richmond, VA: Privately Printed, 1860.

Carson, Jane, ed. *We Were There: Descriptions of Williamsburg, 1699-1859.* Charlottesville: The University Press of Virginia, 1965.

Clark, William B., ed. *Naval Documents of the American Revolution*, Vol. 1-4, Washington, D.C., 1964-68.

Cresswell, Nicholas. *The Journal of Nicholas Cresswell* . The Dial Press: NY, 1974.

Davies, K. G., ed. *Documents of the American Revolution: 1770-1783.* Vols. 8-20. Irish University Press, 1975-1979.

Denny, Ebenezer. *Military Journal of Major Ebenezer Denny.* Philadelphia: J.B. Lippincott and Co., 1859.

Feltman, William. *Journal of Lt. William Feltman of the First Pennsylvania Regiment, 1781-1782.* New York Times & Arno Press, 1969.

Fitzpatrick, John C., ed., *The Writings of George Washington from the Original Manuscript Sources, 1745-1799.* Vol. 23. U.S. Government Printing Office, 1937.

Force, Peter, ed. *American Archives, Fourth Series.* Vols. 2-6. Washington D.C.: M. St. Clair Clarke and Peter Force, 1848.

Force, Peter, ed. *American Archives, Fifth Series*. Vols. 1-3. Washington D.C.: M. St. Clair Clarke and Peter Fore, 1848-1853.

Ford, Worthington, C., ed. *Journals of the Continental Congress, 1774-1789*. Vols. 1-21. Washington, D.C.: U.S. Government Printing Office, 1904-1912.

Gilpin, William, ed. *Memoirs of Josias Rogers, Esq., Commander of His Majesty's Ship Quebec*. London: T. Cadell and W. Davies Strand, 1808.

Graham, James J., ed. *Memoir of General Samuel Graham with Notices of the Campaigns in Which he was Engaged from 1779 to 1801*. Edinburgh: R. & R. Clark, 1862.

Hayes, John T., ed., *A Gentleman of Fortune, The Diary of Baylor Hill, First Continental Light Dragoons, 1777-1781*. Vol. 2. Saddlebagg Press, 1995.

Hening, William W., ed. *The Statutes at Large Being a Collection of all the Laws of Virginia.* Vol. 9-10. Richmond: J. & G. Cochran, 1821-22.

Idzerda, Stanley J., ed. *LaFayette in the Age of the American Revolution: Selected Letters and Papers, 1776-1790.* Vol. 4. Ithaca and London: Cornell University Press, 1981.

Kennedy, John Pendleton, ed. "*Journal of the House of Burgesses*: *1773-1776*. Richmond: VA, 1905.

Laughton, John K., ed. *The Journal of Rear-Admiral Bartholomew James*. London: Navy Records Society, 1896.

Lee, Charles. Lee Papers, Vols. 1-2. New York: New-York Historical Society Publication Fund, 1872.

Martin, Joseph Plum. *Private Yankee Doolittle*. Harrisonburg, PA: Eastern Acorn Press, 1962.

Mays, David John, ed. *The Letters and Papers of Edmund Pendleton, 1734-1803.* Vol. 1, Charlottesville, VA: University Press of Virginia, 1967.

McIlwaine, H. R., ed. *Journals of the Council of State of* Virginia. Vols. 1-2. Richmond, 1931-32.

McIlwaine, H. R., ed. *Official Letters of the Governors of the State of Virginia.* Vol. 1. Richmond: Davis Bottom, Superintendent of Public Printing, 1926.

Morgan, William J., ed. *Naval Documents of the American Revolution.* Vol. 5. Washington D.C.: U.S. Government Printing Office, 1970.

Muhlenberg, Henry. *The Life of Major-General Peter Muhlenberg*. Philadelphia: Cary and Hart, 1849.

Purdie, Alexander. "Proceedings of the House of Delegates, October 11, 1776," *Journal of the House of Delegates of Virginia*. vol. 3. Williamsburg: Alexander Purdie, 1776.

Rice, Howard C. and Anne S.K. Brown, trans. and eds. *The American Campaigns of Rochambeau's Army, 1780*-83. Vol. 1-2. Princeton, NJ and Providence, RI: Princeton University Press, Brown University Press, 1972.

Rochambeau, Count de. *Memoirs of the Marshall Count de Rochambeau.* New York Times & Arno Press, 1971.

Rutland, Robert A, ed. *The Papers of George Mason.* Vol. 1. Chapel Hill: University of North Carolina Press, 1970.

Sandor, Gregory, *Journal of the Public Store, 1775-1776*, (2015)

Shepard, E. Lee, ed. *Marching to Victory: Capt. Benjamin Bartholomew's Diary of the Yorktown Campaign, May 1781 to March 178*1. Richmond: Virginia Historical Society, 2002.

Showman, Richard K., ed. *The Papers of General Nathanael Greene*. Vol. 7. Chapel Hill: The University of North Carolina Press, 1994.

Simcoe, Lt. Col. John. *A Journal of the Operations of the Queen's Rangers, from the end of the year 1777 to the Conclusion of the Late American War.* 1789.

Tarleton, Banastre. *A History of the Campaigns of 1780 and 1781 in the Southern Provinces of North America.* London: T. Cadell, in the Strand, 1787.

Thacher, James. *Military Journal of the American Revolution.* Gansevoort, NY: Corner House Historical Publications, 1998.

Tustin, Joseph, ed. *Diary of the American War: A Hessian Journal*. New Haven: Yale University Press, 1979.

Van Schreeven, William J., Robert L. Scribner, and Brent Tarter, eds., *Revolutionary Virginia: The Road to Independence.* Vols. 1-7. University Press of Virginia, 1973-1983.

Wilcox, William B., ed. *The American Rebellion: Sir Henry Clinton's Narrative of His Campaigns, 1775-1782*. Vol. 2. New Haven: Yale University Press, 1954.

Unpublished

"Charles Dabney to William Wirt, Dec. 21, 1805," *Papers of Patrick Henry* Rockefeller Library CWF, Microfilm.

Inventory and Appraisement of the Estate of Peyton Randolph Esq. in York County taken January 5th, 1776.

Armee de Rochambeau, 1782, Carte des environs de Williamsburg en Virginia ou les armees froncoise et americaine ont camps en Septembre 1781, Map Collection, Library of Congress.

"Embarkation Return for the Following Corps, December 11, 1780, New York," *Sir Henry Clinton Papers*. 113:15, University of Michigan, William L. Clements Library.

Posey, Thomas. *Revolutionary War Journal, Thomas Posey Papers.* Indiana Historical Society Library, Indianapolis, IN.

Articles

Anderson, D. R., ed., "The Letters of Colonel William Woodford, Colonel Robert Howe, and General Charles Lee to Edmund Pendleton," *Richmond College Historical Papers*. Richmond, VA: June, 1915.

Brock, R. A., ed. "The Orderly Book of the Company of Captain George Stubblefield, Fifth Virginia Regiment, from March 3 to July 10, 1776," *Collections of the Virginia Historical Society*. New Series, Vol. 6. Richmond, VA: 1888.

Egle, William H., ed. "Diary of Captain James Duncan of Colonel Moses Hazen's Regiment in the Yorktown Campaign, 1781," *Pennsylvania Archives, 2nd Series*. vol. 15, 1890.

Fuss, Norman. "Prelude to Rebellion: Dunmore's Raid on the Williamsburg Magazine," *Journal of the American Revolution*. Online.

MacMaster, Richard K., ed. "The Journal of Dr. Robert Honyman, April 17 – November 25, 1781," *Virginia Magazine of History and Biography*. 79, no. 4, October 1971.

"Major General Mathew to General Sir Henry Clinton, May 16, 1779," *William and Mary Quarterly, Second Series.* Vol. 12, No. 3, July 1932.

Riley, Edward M., ed., "St George Tucker's Journal of the Siege of Yorktown, 1781," *The William & Mary Quarterly.* vol. 5. no. 3, July, 1948.

Stevens, John Austen, ed. "The Southern Campaign, 1781: From Guildford Courthouse to the Siege of York: Narrated in the Letters from Judge St George Tucker to his Wife, July 11, 1781," *The Magazine of American History.* Vol. 7. July, 1881.

Tarter, Brent, ed. "The Orderly Book of the Second Virginia Regiment: September 27, 1775 – April 15, 1776," *The Virginia Magazine of History and Biography.* Vol. 85, No. 2, April, 1997.

Secondary Sources

Barhart, John D., ed., *Henry Hamilton and George Rogers Clark in the American Revolution with the Unpublished Journals of Lieut. Gov. Henry Hamilton.* Crawfordsville, IN: R. E. Banta, 1951.

Burk, John. *The History of Virginia from Its First Settlement to the Present Day.* Vol. 2. Petersburg, VA: Dickson & Pescud, 1805.

Carson, Jane. *James Innes and His Brothers of the F.H.C.* Charlottesville: University Press of Virginia, 1965.

Commager, Henry S., and Richard B. Morris, *The Spirit of Seventy-Six*. Edison, NJ: Castle Books, 2002.

Greene, Jerome A. *The Guns of Independence: The Siege of Yorktown, 1781.* El Dorado Hills, CA: Savas Beatie, 2005.

Johnston, Henry P. *The Yorktown Campaign and the Surrender of Cornwallis, 1781.* 1881: Ft. Washington, PA: Eastern National, 1997.

Kranish, Michael. *Flight from Monticello: Thomas Jefferson at War*. Oxford: Oxford University Press, 2010.

Lee, Henry. *The Revolutionary War Memoirs of General Henry* Lee. New York: Da Capo Press, 1998.

Lee, Nell Moore. *Patriot Above Profit: A portrait of Thomas Nelson, Jr....,* Nashville, TN: Rutledge Hill Press, 1988.

Namier, Lewis and John Brooks. *The History of Parliament: The House of Commons, 1754-1790.* (Online). https://www.historyofparliamentonline.org/volume/1754-1790/survey/iii-members.

Selby. John E. *Dunmore.* Virginia Independence Bicentennial Commission, 1977.

Selby, John. *The Revolution in Virginia: 1775-1783.* Colonial Williamsburg Foundation, 1988.

Slaughter, Reverend Philip. *A History of St. Mark's Parish: Culpeper County Virginia*. 1877.

Stedman, Charles. *The History of the Origin, Progress, and Termination of the American War*, Vol. 2. London: 1794.

Tyler, Lyon G., ed. "The Williamsburg Companies," *Tyler's Quarterly Historical and Genealogical Magazine*, Vol. 9. Richmond, VA, 1928.

Tyler, Lyon G., *Williamsburg, the Old Capital*. Richmond, VA: Whittet & Shepperson, 1907.

Ward, Harry M. and Harold E. Greer, Jr. *Richmond during the Revolution, 1775-83*. Charlottesville: University Press of Virginia, 1977.

Whitridge, Arnold. *Rochambeau*. New York: Macmillan Co., 1965.

Wirt, William. *Sketches in the Life and Character of Patrick Henry.* Philadelphia, 1817.

Colonial Williamsburg Research Reports

Bullock, Helen. *Public Gaol Historical Report: Block 27, Building 2, Lot 1.* Colonial Williamsburg Foundation Library Research Report Series 1511, John D. Rockefeller Jr., Library, 1930-34.

Carson, Jane. *Lady Dunmore in Virginia*. Colonial Williamsburg Foundation Library Research Report Series, John D. Rockefeller Jr., Library, 1962.

Department of Research, Colonial Williamsburg Foundation. *General Description of Williamsburg: Compiled from Primary Source Material and Chronologically Arranged.* Department of Research and Record Colonial Williamsburg, 1942.

Department of Research, Colonial Williamsburg Foundation. *Prominent Colonial Leaders Associated with Williamsburg*. Colonial Williamsburg Foundation Library Research Report Series 140, John D. Rockefeller Jr., Library.

Foss, Robert. *James Anderson Archeological Report, Block 10, Building 22, Lot 18*. Colonial Williamsburg Foundation Library Research Report Series 1227, John D. Rockefeller Jr., Library, 1977.

Gilman, Carolyn. *Landmarks and Neighborhoods in Eighteenth-Century Williamsburg: A Feasibility Study*. Colonial Williamsburg Foundation Library Research Report Series 405, John D. Rockefeller Jr., Library, 2009.

Goodwin, Mary. *Governors who lived in the Palace*. Colonial Williamsburg Foundation Library Research Report Series 220, John D. Rockefeller Jr., Library, 1955.

Goodwin, Mary. *Clothing and Accoutrements of the Officers and Soldiers of the Virginia Forces, 1775-1780: From the Records of the Public Store at Williamsburg.* Colonial Williamsburg Foundation Library Research Report Series 179, John D. Rockefeller Jr., Library, 1962.

Goodwin, Mary. *Washington in Williamsburg.* Colonial Williamsburg Foundation Library Research Report Series RR0049, John D. Rockefeller Jr., Library, 1954.

Goodwin, W.A.R., *House History File, George Wythe House Historical Report.* Colonial Williamsburg Foundation Library Research Report Series 1484, 1938.

Hamrick, Max. *Williamsburg Manufactory: Revised and Expanded from the 1957 Report of Mills Brown.* Colonial Williamsburg Foundation Library Research Report Series 406, John D. Rockefeller Jr., Library, 2006.

Harris, Collier. *Public Gaol Historical Report: Block 27, Building 2.* Colonial Williamsburg Foundation Library Research Report Series 1628, John D. Rockefeller Jr., Library, 1971.

McCartney, Martha W. *Williamsburg Cultural Resources Map Project: City of Williamsburg.* Colonial Williamsburg Foundation Library Research Report Series 381, John D. Rockefeller Jr., Library, 2003.

Middleton, Arthur P., and Edward M. Riley. *The Capitol: A Manual of Interpretation Designed Principally for the Use of the Hostesses and Escorts of Colonial Williamsburg.* Colonial Williamsburg Foundation Library Research Report Series 205, 1959.

Nicholls, Michael. *Aspects of the African American Experience in Eighteenth Century Williamsburg and Norfolk.* Colonial Williamsburg Foundation Library Research Report Series 330, 1990.

Poirer, Noel. *The Williamsburg Public Armory: A Historical Study, Block 10, Building 22F.* Colonial Williamsburg Foundation Library Research Report Series 406, John D. Rockefeller Jr., Library, 2003.

Ragland, Herbert, S., Department of Research. *The Governor's Palace: Historical Notes.* Colonial Williamsburg Foundation Library Research Report Series 219, 1930.

Schupp, Katherine W. *Anderson's Blacksmith Shop: A Case for the Tinsmith Among the Anvils, Block 10, Area G.* Colonial Williamsburg Foundation Library Research Report Series 1690, John D. Rockefeller Jr., Library, 2003.

Soltow, James H. *The Occupational Structure of Williamsburg in 1775.* Colonial Williamsburg Foundation Library Research Report Series 128, Colonial Williamsburg Foundation, 1990.

Stephenson, Mary A. *George Pitt House (LT) Historical Report, Block 18-2, Building 48*. Colonial Williamsburg Foundation Library Research Report Series 1391, 1960.

Townsend, Raymond. *Peyton Randolph Historical Report, Block 28, Building 6, Lot 207 & 237*. Colonial Williamsburg Foundation Library Research Report Series 1537, 1967.

Walsh, Lorena S., Ann Smart Martin, and Joanne Bowen. *Provisioning Early American Towns, The Chesapeake: A Multidisciplinary Case Study: Final Performance Report.* Colonial Williamsburg Foundation Library Research Report Series 0404, 1997.

Newspapers

Caledonian Mercury, October 10, 1781.
Dixon and Hunter, *Virginia Gazette, Supplement* December 8, 1774.
Dixon and Hunter, *Virginia Gazette,* January 21, 1775.
Dixon and Hunter, *Virginia Gazette*, June 10, 1775.
Dixon and Hunter, *Virginia Gazette,* February 4, 1775.
Dixon & Hunter, *Virginia Gazette*, January 14, 1775.
Dixon and Hunter, *Virginia Gazette*, April 1, 1775.
Dixon and Hunter, *Virginia Gazette,* June 24, 1775.
Dixon and Hunter, *Virginia Gazette,* October 28, 1775.
Dixon and Hunter, *Virginia Gazette*, August 24, 1776.
Dixon and Hunter, *Virginia Gazette*, December 13, 1776.
Dixon and Hunter, *Virginia Gazette*, March 21, 1777.
Dixon, *Virginia Gazette*, May 16, 1777.
Dixon and Hunter, *Virginia Gazette*, May 30, 1777.

Dixon and Hunter, *Virginia Gazette*, August 22, 1777.
Dixon and Hunter, *Virginia Gazette*, October 31, 1777.
Dixon and Hunter, *Virginia Gazette*, May 15, 1778.
Dixon and Nicolson, *Virginia Gazette*, February 26, 1779.
Dixon and Nicolson, *Virginia Gazette*, March 19, 1779.
Dixon and Nicolson, *Virginia Gazette*, June 19, 1779.
Dixon and Nicolson, *Virginia Gazette*, January 22, 1780.
Dixon and Nicolson, *Virginia Gazette*, February 5, 1780.
Dixon and Nicolson, *Virginia Gazette*, March 25, 1780.
Pennsylvania Packet, July 21, 1781.
Pinkney, *Virginia Gazette*, March 30, 1775.
Pinkney, *Virginia Gazette*, April 13, 1775.
Pinkney, *Virginia Gazette*, June 1, 1775.
Pinkney, *Virginia Gazette*, June 8, 1775.
Pinkney, *Virginia Gazette*, September 7, 1775.
Pinkney, *Virginia Gazette*, October 12, 1775.
Pinkney, *Virginia Gazette,* October 26, 1775.
Pinkney, *Virginia Gazette,* November 2, 1775.
Pinkney, *Virginia Gazette*, November 30, 1775.
Purdie, *Virginia Gazette,* February 3, 1775.
Purdie, *Virginia Gazette Supplement*, March 31, 1775.
Purdie, *Virginia Gazette,* April 14, 1775.
Purdie, *Virginia Gazette Supplement,* June 9, 1775.
Purdie, *Virginia Gazette Supplement,* April 21, 1775.
Purdie, *Virginia Gazette Supplement,* April 28, 1775.
Purdie, *Virginia Gazette Supplement,* June 30, 1775.
Purdie, *Virginia Gazette*, July 7, 1775.
Purdie, *Virginia Gazette Supplement.* July 14, 1775.
Purdie, *Virginia Gazette,* August 25, 1775.
Purdie, *Virginia Gazette*, October 6, 1775.
Purdie, *Virginia Gazette*, August 4, 1775.

Purdie, *Virginia Gazette*, Williamsburg, January 5, 1776.
Purdie, *Virginia Gazette*, March 1, 1776.
Purdie, *Virginia Gazette*, April 5, 1776.
Purdie, *Virginia Gazette*, April 19, 1776.
Purdie, "*Virginia Gazette,* Williamsburg, April 5, 1776.
Purdie, *Virginia Gazette*, May 17, 1776.
Purdie, *Virginia Gazette*, May 24, 1776.
Purdie, *Virginia Gazette*, July 26, 1776.
Purdie, *Virginia Gazette*, August 2, 1776.
Purdie, "*Virginia Gazette*, August 23, 1776.
Purdie, *Virginia Gazette Supplement,* December 20, 1776.
Purdie, *Virginia Gazette*, August 9, 1776.
Purdie, *Virginia Gazette*, October 11, 1776.
Purdie, *Virginia Gazette*, October 18, 1776.
Purdie, *Virginia Gazette*, January 5, 1776.
Purdie, *Virginia Gazette*, August 15, 1777.
Purdie, *Virginia Gazette*, July 25, 1777.
Purdie, *Virginia Gazette*, October 31, 1777.
Purdie, *Virginia Gazette*, November 21, 1777.
Purdie and Dixon, *Virginia Gazette,* June 2, 1774.
Purdie and Dixon, *Virginia Gazette,* July 14, 1774.
Purdie and Dixon, *Virginia Gazette,* August 11, 1774.
Purdie and Dixon, *Virginia Gazette,* July 21, 1774.
Purdie and Dixon, *Virginia Gazette,* July 28, 1774.
Purdie and Dixon, *Virginia Gazette,* December 22, 1774.
Royal, *Virginia Gazette*, October 25, 1765.

Index

H

O

P

Q

R

S

CPSIA information can be obtained
at www.ICGtesting.com
Printed in the USA
JSHW020149180323
39032JS00002B/76

9 780788 444043